CRYPTOGRAMS
ON THE
FLIP SIDE

LESLIE BILLIG
& SHAWN KENNEDY

STERLING
INNOVATION
A Division of Sterling Publishing Co., Inc.
New York

see 95

Four letter words that start & finish with the same letters are usually the word: THAT & ELSE WERE etc

the letter that occurs most often in the puzzle is usually E. count!

A single letter can only be either A or I (naturally)

Finish #93!

2 4 6 8 10 9 7 5 3 1

Published by Sterling Publishing Co., Inc.
387 Park Avenue South, New York, NY 10016

The material in this book has been excerpted from the following Sterling Publishing Co., Inc. titles:
Mighty Mini Crypto-Quotes © 1999 by Leslie Billig
Funny Cryptograms © 2003 by Shawn Kennedy

Distributed in Canada by Sterling Publishing
c/o Canadian Manda Group, 165 Dufferin Street
Toronto, Ontario, Canada M6K 3H6
Distributed in the United Kingdom by GMC Distribution Services
Castle Place, 166 High Street, Lewes, East Sussex, England BN7 1XU
Distributed in Australia by Capricorn Link (Australia) Pty. Ltd.
P.O. Box 704, Windsor, NSW 2756, Australia

Design by StarGraphics Studio

Printed in China

Sterling ISBN-13: 978-1-4027-4689-5
ISBN-10: 1-4027-4689-X

For information about custom editions, special sales, premium and
corporate purchases, please contact Sterling Special Sales
Department at 800-805-5489 or specialsales@sterlingpub.com.

13

SMLMK PMTT GMUGTM FUV PU XU PFBSEY. PMTT PFMC VFOP PU XU OSX PFMH VBTT YDKGKBYM HUD VBPF PFMBK BSEMSDBPH.

—EMUKEM GOPPUS

14

UDD BVFR QYDQSY YHQYPU CDFWYZK AZDB WYBDPZVPR, CTYF UTY BDKU CDFWYZAXS UTGFJ DA VSS GK NXKU TVOGFJ GU.

—CVSUYZ CGFPTYSS

15

P MKZKAVUJI UY YHLKHQK CSH CHVRY SPVF PZZ SUY ZUWK JH AKMHLK CKZZ-RQHCQ, PQF JSKQ CKPVY FPVR DZPYYKY JH PBHUF AKUQD VKMHDQUEKF.

—WVKF PZZKQ

13 K represents R — 14 B represents M — 15 C represents W

13

Never tell people how to do things. Tell them what to do and they will surprise you with their ingenuity.

—George Patton

14

Too many people expect wonders from democracy, when the most wonderful thing of all is just having it.

—Walter Winchell

15

A celebrity is someone who works hard all his life to become well-known, and then wears dark glasses to avoid being recognized.

—Fred Allen

25

AV KVS SCI PVFS PVUDKY PVPIKSF VM VTG
BDUIF MDKA TF JBB RDSCVTS RVGAF?

—PJGZIB PJGZIJT

26

LQRRNI MBI QE DOI MGSGMCR HICQKR GOIZ
XMDOIC DQLI EDMCDE TMDTOQZB VH GQDO
LKDOIC ZMDVCI.

—OMCKNR TKXXQZ

27

KCIISAK YSDNFBCY MXGI TCBQXGC ENX YNA'I
RNDC Q LQA SG QRLNGI QG GSRRE QG
KCIISAK LQFFSCY MXGI TCBQXGC ENX YN.

—UGQ UGQ KQTNF

25 A represents D

26 L represents M

27 E represents Y

25

Do not the most moving moments of our lives find us all without words?

—Marcel Marceau

26

Middle age is the awkward period when Father Time starts catching up with Mother Nature.

—Harold Coffin

27

Getting divorced just because you don't love a man is almost as silly as getting married just because you do.

—Zsa Zsa Gabor

31

EDKXK FXK EMY EDHROI EDFE MHTT VK VKTHKZKC YL FRU SFR MDFEIYKZKX, FRC YRK YL EDKS HI EDFE DK DFI EFJKR EY CXHRJ.

—VYYED EFXJHROEYR

32

Q HDMDPQUJQT JR RWFDYWKX NBW NWT'P DQP QTXPBJTM PBQP ZQT BQHD ZBJEKUDT.

—KQHJK YUDTTDU

33

XHS BVG DNFC V DNYCRNLC VGK, VR RPC CGK HY NR, IGHO LHQC VZHSR HRPCQ JCHJDC RPVG XHS IGHO VZHSR XHSQWCDY.

—ZCQXD LVQIPVL

31 R represents N 32 Z represents C 33 H represents O

31

There are two things that will be believed of any man whatsoever, and one of them is that he has taken to drink.

—Booth Tarkington

32

A vegetarian is somebody who won't eat anything that can have children.

—David Brenner

33

You can live a lifetime and, at the end of it, know more about other people than you know about yourself.

—Beryl Markham

34

GCHNT KDVTFQ NSD JGD MTWR ESDNJCSDQ
MT DNSJG JGNJ NWWMU JGDVS EGVWOSDT
JM EMHD KNEP GMHD.

—KVWW EMQKR

35

W VJMJU RQIYX IVXJUTOBVX GQA OAQ FJV
RBV AUWOJ B SQQL OQEJOGJU; OQ FJ
OGBO'T YWLJ OGUJJ ZJQZYJ EJOOWVE
OQEJOGJU OQ GBMJ B SBSD.

—JMJYDV ABIEG

36

BRK BDSFVMK YCBR MCPK CI BRK PJAB MJIK
CA BRJB XSF OKB BS BRK SBRKD KIN CI JI
JYPFM RFDDX.

—USRI UKIAKI

34 M represents O 35 G represents H 36 D represents R

34

Human beings are the only creatures on earth that allow their children to come back home.

—Bill Cosby

35

I never could understand how two men can write a book together; to me that's like three people getting together to have a baby.

—Evelyn Waugh

36

The trouble with life in the fast lane is that you get to the other end in an awful hurry.

—John Jensen

40

OQ CGW TFDYOV YOPWR ISF, ISF'BW LSSH. RGZPWRTWZBW AZR Z VSKKSM, HSAM-CS-WZBCG ABOCWB OM GOR HZI.

—KOVPWI RTOYYZMW

41

KXEY XF YIFXYU MJIP THB'Q MJXPS; IKK MJIM XF PYZYFFIUT XF MH IZZYGM MJY XAGHFFXDKY, QH CXMJHBM MJY XPQXFGYPFIDKY, IPQ DYIU MJY XPMHKYUIDKY.

—SIMJKYYP PHUUXF

42

O YG PBMV Y FJUMOZ KBAKNAYOBKN RQP QYW JBCKNWAPPC QOW AOGK.

—FYUMP FOZYWWP

40 C represents T | 41 Z represents C | 42 B represents N

40

If the public likes you, you're good. Shakespeare was a common, down-to-earth writer in his day.

—Mickey Spillane

41

Life is easier than you'd think; all that is necessary is to accept the impossible, do without the indispensable, and bear the intolerable.

—Kathleen Norris

42

I am only a public entertainer who has understood his time.

—Pablo Picasso

43

ZFKLLKX ML CWK EQT JWR, WQUMTY TRCWMTY CR LQD, QZLCQMTL AGRE YMUMTY JRGXD KUMXKTOK RA CWK AQOC.

—YKRGYK KFMRC

44

OZHUFUWD UD RZF S ISE OLZMJDDUZR. UM XZP DPWWJJE FKJLJ SLJ TSRX LJVSLED; UM XZP EUDNLSWJ XZPLDJHM XZP WSR SHVSXD VLUFJ S IZZG.

—LZRSHE LJSNSR

45

CNU YZAGC ZV SAJAGF, QGW ZV IUAGF QG ZYCAPAEC, AE CZ IU VZZSAEN UGZDFN CZ IUSAUJU CNU IUEC AE BUC CZ HZPU.

—YUCUL DECAGZJ

43 X represents D

44 W represents C

45 I represents B

43

Blessed is the man who, having nothing to say, abstains from giving wordy evidence of the fact.

—George Eliot

44

Politics is not a bad profession. If you succeed there are many rewards; if you disgrace yourself you can always write a book.

—Ronald Reagan

45

The point of living, and of being an optimist, is to be foolish enough to believe the best is yet to come.

—Peter Ustinov

46

BKSMSBUTM LOYINW WIRQIC, LOU YU BSX LT URMX NRQX QYUK YXBMTNYLIT WQYHUXTWW.

—HSYUK LSINQYX

47

ZHSZTAZDPZ AU DMJ OQKJ QKSSZDU JM VMF; AJ AU OQKJ VMF WM OAJQ OQKJ QKSSZDU JM VMF.

—KEWMFU QFHEZV

48

FTN NSDYNDF USG FH IHWLYWIN ZG JYXD FTSF FTNG XHW'F QNSPPG WNNX DHZNFTYWE YD FH ENF YF OHQ FTNZ.

—MHSW IHPPYWD

46 I represents L

47 O represents W

48 X represents D

46

Character builds slowly, but it can be torn down with incredible swiftness.

—Faith Baldwin

47

Experience is not what happens to you; it is what you do with what happens to you.

—Aldous Huxley

48

The easiest way to convince my kids that they don't really need something is to get it for them.

—Joan Collins

49

NII R QWWO AK JNHW N PKJWOU RM N DNZH, N DKIRPWJNQ, NQO N DZWAAU SRZI.

—PYNZIRW PYNDIRQ

50

S ASY EZDWYO INPPWYD MWO GWOBUA PZZPM PMZ CWQOP PWAZ MZ EWPZO UCC AUQZ PMSY MZ ISY IMZG.

—MZQE ISZY

51

AZCINEWQQH, L XBLEO LJ W UNVWE BWIE'X VZX XBZ CLYBX VWE GH XBZ XLVZ IBZ'I XUZEXH-JNRC, IBZ VWH GZ QRPOH.

—SZGNCWB OZCC

49 W represents E

50 U represents O

51 V represents M

49

All I need to make a comedy is a park, a policeman, and a pretty girl.

—Charlie Chaplin

50

A man begins cutting his wisdom teeth the first time he bites off more than he can chew.

—Herb Caen

51

Personally, I think if a woman hasn't met the right man by the time she's twenty-four, she may be lucky.

—Deborah Kerr

52

P LJQH DR ARKY PE N BPKQ ZIHKNED BNMDRKI. IRL MRLFHE'D XNKY NEIAZQKQ EQNK DZQ XFNMQ.

—JDQCQE AKPWZD

53

QENUN YUN QIK IYCZ KD ZGUNYBTSF OTFEQ: QK VN QEN PYSBON KU QEN WTUUKU QEYQ UNDONPQZ TQ.

—NBTQE IEYUQKS

54

C QXZI HJ JXKIXOI YLX UIZJHJMJ HO LXDGHOR LHJ XYO PHIYJ CTMIZ YI LCPI IODHRLMIOIG LHK YHML XWZJ.

—KCDFXDK TXZQIJ

52 L represents U

53 O represents L

54 M represents T

52

I used to work in a fire hydrant factory. You couldn't park anywhere near the place.

—Steven Wright

53

There are two ways of spreading light: to be the candle or the mirror that reflects it.

—Edith Wharton

54

A bore is someone who persists in holding his own views after we have enlightened him with ours.

—Malcolm Forbes

55

PML POCIAKL RBPM PML QOCHBP DJDPLX
MYD YKRYJD ALLG PMYP BP BD MBFMKJ
IGQOCHBPYAKL PC XCDP QLCQKL.

—L.A. RMBPL

56

SYM SD ROM SNAMGR OJZLY YMMAG KG
OLPKYF GSZMSYM RS ISYAMW IOMWM HSJ
LWM IOMY HSJ ASY'R ESZM OSZM LR YKFOR.

—ZLWFLWMR ZMLA

57

DEJ ZOWA DEQOV DEUD GUYJG HG SKZF DEJ
PHKJUHMKUMA QG QDG QOJSSQMQJOMA.

—JHVJOJ FMMUKDEA

55 R represents W   56 Z represents M   57 G represents S

55

The trouble with the profit system has always been that it is highly unprofitable to most people.

—E.B. White

56

One of the oldest human needs is having someone to wonder where you are when you don't come home at night.

—Margaret Mead

57

The only thing that saves us from the bureaucracy is its inefficiency.

—Eugene McCarthy

61

NRQDUHT MY AMLUS FXBKIQDU TXMLKI QDRKBOD HXRH YDC NDMNKD CBKK YBUI HXDBQ FXBKIQDU RT DUFXRUHBUS RT HXDA IM.

—VRQVRQR CRKHDQT

62

OFMDG MTMIGW SDJM SM UYEMG DIV BDCS; EG EW HICZ GFEKCMW GQDG EFFEGDGM SZ IMFTMW.

—UYMMI TEBGHFED

63

DV ODZ WRPPZS JZTFKYV ZSDVTM UVMSTZIM SDV ATKUFV ZYVT ODKWD DV DKHMVXJ HEMS BRMM.

—FVZTFV DVTAVTS

61 I represents D | 62 T represents V | 63 O represents W

61

Parents of young children should realize that few people will find their children as enchanting as they do.

—Barbara Walters

62

Great events make me quiet and calm; it is only trifles that irritate my nerves.

—Queen Victoria

63

He who cannot forgive others destroys the bridge over which he himself must pass.

—George Herbert

64

NAQ DMH BE ABCH HYHWGLUBIM HAEH. LN SDCH D EZVVHEE NJ BL, GNZ'YH MNL LN ELDWL GNZIM.

—JWHQ DELDBWH

65

QYQRHZ YFH YEXYDZ VBFH NFBPQEH NKYO DBP NKBPUKN—YOS VBFH XBOSHFJPE.

—LKYFEHZ BZUBBS

66

XLI JB RM XLI CJCIO DJRB "GRU DJKI. KJDX FIIT." FLP JBYIOXRDI? R JKOIJBP VRDDIB RX. XLIP'OI EHDX OHGGRMU RX RM.

—PJTZY DVROMZAA

64 L represents T

65 D represents Y

66 G represents B

64

Old age is like everything else. To make a success of it, you've got to start young.

—Fred Astaire

65

Babies are always more trouble than you thought—and more wonderful.

—Charles Osgood

66

The ad in the paper said "Big Sale. Last Week." Why advertise? I already missed it.

They're just rubbing it in.

—Yakov Smirnoff

67

HP RUMT YHPFUAP TISHKR PFIP SUA TFUACE KMNMD FINM QUDM OFHCEDMK PFIK SUA FINM OID YHKEUYT.

—MDQI LUQLMOX

68

HAUHTA SKU SUWO IVEEVRQ XUSR QAE HJVX DUWA EKJR HAUHTA SKU SUWO IEJRXVRQ YH.

—UQXAR RJIK

69

JA TPMX TPD LTZMS QUKD NVT MJKDE: NQD AJOEN JP VQJLQ NT HUID TPD'E HJENUIDE, UPS NQD EDLTPS JP VQJLQ NT WOTAJN YX NQDH.

—S.Q. MUVODPLD

67 S represents Y | 68 E represents T | 69 P represents N

67

It goes without saying that you should never have more children than you have car windows.

—Erma Bombeck

68

People who work sitting down get paid more than people who work standing up.

—Ogden Nash

69

If only one could have two lives: the first in which to make one's mistakes, and the second in which to profit by them.

—D.H. Lawrence

70

CVHK NHJNOH RHHN ZHOODKF EJW ZVYZ EJW IYK'Z QJ Y ZVDKF, EJW RDKQ JB ODRH ZJ ZAE DZ.

—LYAFYAHZ IVYGH GLDZV

71

MKDSLQTFXQ KVVUKCD FX AU PLYYUR MLFS FMX OLQRD XP VXYLFLELKQD—FSXDU FCGLQT FX TUF KQ LQZUDFLTKFLXQ DFKCFUR, KQR FSXDU FCGLQT FX TUF XQU DFXVVUR.

—UKCY MLYDXQ

72

DONT BE HUMBLE YOURE NOT THAT GREAT

ADZ'F UH MCVUBH. QDC'TH ZDF FMJF ITHJF.

GOLDA MEYR

—IDBAJ VHST

70 D represents I | 71 S represents H | 72 M represents H

70

When people keep telling you that you can't do a thing, you kind of like to try it.

—Margaret Chase Smith

71

Washington appears to be filled with two kinds of politicians—those trying to get an investigation started, and those trying to get one stopped.

—Earl Wilson

72

Don't be humble. You're not that great.

—Golda Meir

73

AGR UKORMNDCYZ GYCL DW BDIRMCKRCA HYC CRIRM MROZYHR AGR GRZOUCB GYCL DW Y CRUBGTDM.

—GSTRMA G. GSKOGMRP

74

FJBIWKG AC T CAGSG FRJBIMR ERAQR EG CAXF BIJ TQLITAPFTPQGC. FRBCG FBB WAM FB ZTCC FRJBIMR TJG BIJ XJAGPHC.

—TJKGPG XJTPQAC

75

JQVE UVFF YDBCVX JQD FCXW NH JQD HYDD NXFZ EN FNXO CE VJ VE JQD QNBD NH JQD PYCLD.

—DFBDY WCLVE

73 C represents N

74 J represents R

75 N represents O

73

The impersonal hand of government can never replace the helping hand of a neighbor.

—Hubert H. Humphrey

74

Trouble is a sieve through which we sift our acquaintances. Those too big to pass through are our friends.

—Arlene Francis

75

This will remain the land of the free only so long as it is the home of the brave.

—Elmer Davis

76

MJ ZAX EYL QIID ZAXU PIYC NPIL YVV YTAXH ZAX YUI VAOMLF HPIMUO, MH'O BXOH DAOOMTVI ZAX PYKIL'H FUYODIC HPI OMHXYHMAL.

—BIYL QIUU

77

UYO HODXHQXNPO UYSJV XNFKU GYXQOGBOXHO SG UYXU YO HOXPPR SG TOHR VFFZ, SJ GBSUO FI XPP UYO BOFBPO EYF GXR YO SG TOHR VFFZ.

—HFNOHU VHXTOG

78

M UMK'H DRO OR OMPL M IRO RY SQKZHGULKO OR BJZOL M JLMIIC YQKKC XRRP.

—LJKLHO GLUZKDBMC

76 D represents P

77 H represents R

78 Y represents F

76

If you can keep your head when all about you are losing theirs, it's just possible you haven't grasped the situation.

—Jean Kerr

77

The remarkable thing about Shakespeare is that he really is very good, in spite of all the people who say he is very good.

—Robert Graves

78

A man's got to take a lot of punishment to write a really funny book.

—Ernest Hemingway

79

TES VLJ RLDFNT HSQWR UBR VBLALVURA EG L XLJ MT BEY BR UARLUD UBEDR YBE VLJ QE JEUBFJW GEA BFX.

—HLXRD Q. XFNRD

80

Z VJMO MOQOEZHZGD. Z VJMO ZM JH LNIV JH TOJDNMH. FNM Z IJD'M HMGT OJMZDX TOJDNMH.

—GAHGD YOQQOH

81

PVQ TQDP CFE XADP TQCJPBYJS PVBFLD BF PVQ RAZSE UCFFAP TQ DQQF AZ QWQF PAJUVQE. PVQH XJDP TQ YQSP RBPV PVQ VQCZP.

—VQSQF GQSSQZ

79 V represents C | 80 T represents P | 81 B represents I

79

You can easily judge the character of a man by how he treats those who can do nothing for him.

—James D. Miles

80

I hate television. I hate it as much as peanuts. But I can't stop eating peanuts.

—Orson Welles

81

The best and most beautiful things in the world cannot be seen or even touched. They must be felt with the heart.

—Helen Keller

82

NWG RO AXEAIMISKI OE FBJW FEXQ OBJJQOOTBV NWQS RD ODRXO BA WIDXQK DWIS NWQS RD DXRQO DE ODRX BA TXRQSKVG TQQVRSM?

—PQXDXISK XBOOQVV

83

WPR IJU TE EYIWWROX JA WT ATTWPR IVN RVFTSOIKR SA QX IAASOJVK SA TE WPR WOSWP TE IV TZJVJTV CR PIBR IYORINX ETOURN IQTSW TSOARYBRA.

—RNJWP AJWCRYY

84

IXLJRIY VXB MZRLW, RG VXB JXOW LX PW CIV YXXU, MRKK WNWZ QXDW XBL CA VXB GRZAL JXOWU.

—KRKKRCI JWKKDCI

82 A represents P

83 V represents N

84 I represents N

82

Why is propaganda so much more successful when it stirs up hatred than when it tries to stir up friendly feeling?

—Bertrand Russell

83

The aim of flattery is to soothe and encourage us by assuring us of the truth of an opinion we have already formed about ourselves.

—Edith Sitwell

84

Nothing you write, if you hope to be any good, will ever come out as you first hoped.

—Lillian Hellman

85

I HAVE FOUND THAT THE BEST WAY TO
B THSD UFCPN WTHW WTD RDEW QHM WF
GIVE ADVICE TO YOUR CHILDREN IS TO
ABSD HNSBZD WF MFCL ZTBONLDP BE WF
FIND OUT WHAT THEY WANT AND THEN
UBPN FCW QTHW WTDM QHPW, HPN WTDP
ADVISE THEM TO DO IT
HNSBED WTDI WF NF BW.

HARRY TRUMAN
—THLLM WLCIHP

86

FAUKR FAUJ DIYIZJ JLI JLWAPLJU ZQH KQUYKDZJKWQU WX JLI YIWYNI ZQH JLI JKFIU.

—PIWDPI PIDULVKQ

87

EPRTEJ-ZWOD UWOD DWWB QRDFSLR VRTRDKIIJ DRZRDQ EW EUR IRTVEU WZ ESBR EUKE SE EKYRQ ZWD EUR LIOG QKTAPSLU EW KDDSFR.

—ZDKT IRGWPSEH

85 M represents Y | 86 K represents I | 87 Z represents F

85

I have found that the best way to give advice to your children is to find out what they want, and then advise them to do it.

—Harry Truman

86

Music must repeat the thoughts and inspirations of the people and the times.

—George Gershwin

87

Twenty-four hour room service generally refers to the length of time that it takes for the club sandwich to arrive.

—Fran Lebowitz

88

WCDT NLVTP BUD YX PKLVI UDT XUPM IL POXUW, YHI IKXCV XBKLXP UVX IVHAM XDTAXPP.

—RLIKXV IXVXPU

89

ISYFY NE OM SKHGO RFMPZYH USNXS XMKZT OMI PY EMZCYT NV RYMRZY UMKZT ENHRZQ TM GE N GTCNEY.

—DMFY CNTGZ

90

YZ KJP NDDE JC GRKYCX SIYCXG RVD XJYCX SJ QD QRB, KJP IRAD R XJJB UIRCUD JZ QDYCX R EVJEIDS.

—YGRRU QRGIDAYG GYCXDV

88 Y represents B

89 R represents P

90 Q represents B

88

Kind words can be short and easy to speak, but their echoes are truly endless.

—Mother Teresa

89

There is no human problem which could not be solved if people would simply do as I advise.

—Gore Vidal

90

If you keep on saying things are going to be bad, you have a good chance of being a prophet.

—Isaac Bashevis Singer

91

XAUWQEXYC ENAAJYQEXLU LGWNJRG DJLLNYC, L-CGQWLC, XYF DJAVUW CLQEZUWC LGU OXP CNAU EJILJWUC JCU FWJAC.

—LQA AEEXWLGP

92

YGN WAZK XR FMZMKACN MQAOGYC XSQD EFXS YGN GMSK YGMY KXNC SXY OZMCF.

—PXGS WNZZD

93

NMLRID DRK SFRQ QFLK ILRT, EXQ QFLK NJT'Q DRK VQ VT NRKQVIL BRTAXRAL.

—ARVB AJNSVT

91 J represents U | 92 A represents I | 93 K represents Y

91

Americans communicate through buttons, T-shirts, and bumper stickers the way some cultures use drums.

—Tim McCarthy

92

The bird of paradise alights only upon the hand that does not grasp.

—John Berry

93

Dreams say what they mean, but they don't say it in daytime language.

—Gail Godwin

94

H KPLLKO AOQOKKPRJ JRZ HJU LTOJ PW H BRRU LTPJB, HJU HW JOSOWWHAD PJ LTO VRKPLPSHK ZRAKU HW WLRAGW PJ LTO VTDWPSHK.

—LTRGHW YOMMOAWRJ

95

M GWD'X URNMRPR MD QD QCXRLNMCR, QNXFWZOF M QH ULMDOMDO Q KFQDOR WC ZDGRLARQL.

—AWWGS QNNRD

96

JR K ZJMFDZ DR DCCDQEGMJEX KCCWKQB, FDM'E CGYY FDZM ELW BLKFW.

—EDV CWEWQB

94 T represents H

95 O represents G

96 Z represents W

94

A little rebellion now and then is a good thing, and as necessary in the political world as storms in the physical.

—Thomas Jefferson

95

I don't believe in an afterlife, although I am bringing a change of underwear.

—Woody Allen

96

If a window of opportunity appears, don't pull down the shade.

—Tom Peters

97

RCRXW TRYRXVFMLY DVGTPN VF FPR LDQ BVNPMLYN, SGF XRDMTMLGNDW BLDDLON FPR YRO.

—PRYXW QVCMQ FPLXRVG

98

THERE IS NO DENYING THE FACT THAT
QKWSW UA JZ HWJXUJR QKW NFVQ QKFQ
WRITERS SHOULD TO READ BUT NOT SEEM
TSUQWSA AKZOMH GW SWFH GOQ JZQ AWWJ.
RARELY ARE THEY A WINSOME SIGHT
SFSWMX FSW QKWX F TUJAZCW AURKQ.

EDNA FERBER
—WHJF NWSGWS

99

H RIYGBS JU LIY H ABSUIL YI DBHL IL VCY H ABSUIL YI RHWB DBHLJLQ CLLBFBUUHSX.

—EISIYGX FHLPJBDE PJUGBS

97 Y represents N

98 J represents N

99 Y represents T

97

Every generation laughs at the old fashions, but religiously follows the new.

—Henry David Thoreau

98

There is no denying the fact that writers should be read but not seen. Rarely are they a winsome sight.

—Edna Ferber

99

A mother is not a person to lean on but a person to make leaning unnecessary.

—Dorothy Canfield Fisher

100

SWUIGSD GO QKWSD QGUI OWBUIFKS JTYGPWKSGT UITU T KGOF GS UIF WJFTS YFMFY QWBYLS'U JBKF.

—KWOO ATJLWSTYL

101

FUT WNP XES DU FUTG ZERS UG FUTG HUKK, HTD FUT WNPPUD XES DU FUTG DFLSZGEDSG. KUUPSG UG XNDSG FUT VTKD GSISNX FUTG DGTS KSXR EP FUTG LNJSK.

—XSUP TGEK

102

EPQCLSI QX UWI RMAYQVIAU UWPU KQOIX XLRRIXX QUX ECPOMS.

—USLVPA RPHMUI

100 Q represents W

101 D represents T

102 Q represents I

100

Nothing is wrong with Southern California that a rise in the ocean level wouldn't cure.

—Ross MacDonald

101

You can lie to your wife or your boss, but you cannot lie to your typewriter. Sooner or later you must reveal your true self in your pages.

—Leon Uris

102

Failure is the condiment that gives success its flavor.

—Truman Capote

103

HOF ZNRH DFEIHYSIM HOYUJR YU HOF CNQMK EQF HOF ZNRH IRFMFRR: XFETNTWR EUK MYMYFR, SNQ YURHEUTF.

—LNOU QIRWYU

104

TG GCZKL C JESD GTBK GE XKCJ C IVEZKS XKCVG. IHG QJCMTSD ESK EN BM CJIHBL YCS XKJQ.

—NVCSZ LTSCGVC

105

OEE VBABEBYODBUM ZON SJUI DBIC DU DBIC RCVUIC O DZBM VJTND UACJ O AUEVOMU US JCAUETDBUM.

—ZOACEUVH CEEBN

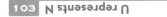

103 U represents N | 104 I represents B | 105 A represents V

103

The most beautiful things in the world are the most useless: peacocks and lilies, for instance.

—John Ruskin

104

It takes a long time to heal a broken heart. But playing one of my albums can help.

—Frank Sinatra

105

All civilization has from time to time become a thin crust over a volcano of revolution.

—Havelock Ellis

106

HSJ MRTOA KV CJXRTJ DRN, GIA DRN IJJA IRH HGWJ KH RT OJGPJ KH GV KH MGV MSJI DRN QGYJ KI.

—BGYJV CGOAMKI

107

VSWU PUW BTCB ISTI T VDEIWD EB QTBSEPUTKRW PUW HDTJIEJTRRC TRVTCB NWTUB ISTI SW EB TFNEDWF KC HWPHRW XUFWD ISEDIC.

—MWPDMW PDVWRR

108

DSESAT KY D YPDYHT XHGGHCPV KAAPVKDEPGQ LQ GHHOKTF XHZCDZV EH YRZKTF.

—VHSF GDZYHT

106 D represents Y | 107 V represents W | 108 G represents L

106

The world is before you, and you need not take it or leave it as it was when you came in.

—James Baldwin

107

When one says that a writer is fashionable one practically always means that he is admired by people under thirty.

—George Orwell

108

Autumn is a season followed immediately by looking forward to spring.

—Doug Larson

109

YNH TZBN NQIH Q FQRRZUJ XUT MQTKQZJR QR GZIHGD QR ZY ZR FUZJYGHRR.

—XTQJBUZRH RQKQJ

110

HXX ZLS HCJXUCUM HLU IRXREFNHX. CJUT MZUHV UEFXRMJ HEB ZLSQHERCT.

—FSLBRU JSKU

111

OZXMAOE AQ UZYJ HALLAWPVX, SOH XMJYJLZYJ UZYJ GYJWAZPQ, XMSO XZ DJ SDVJ XZ HJWAHJ.

—OSGZVJZO

109 T represents R | 110 E represents N | 111 H represents D

109

The rich have a passion for bargains as lively as it is pointless.

—Françoise Sagan

110

All pro athletes are bilingual. They speak English and profanity.

—Gordie Howe

111

Nothing is more difficult, and therefore more precious, than to be able to decide.

—Napoleon

112

SK SH G WGAJIW BNNM ASJW SJWIIW KVGK LGJ'K KVSJU NZ GK EIGHK KTN TGFH NZ HBIEESJQ GJF TNMW.

—GJWMIT RGLUHNJ

113

XDEVLZVE XQV X YIIM ALNBJVLZV AL BITV XLM GVBO UVVO AH DQAYGH XLM MVBAZXHV.

—QIDVQH BIJAE EHVTVLEIL

114

AWMFPCGV KD CPG DPUVCGDC XKDCWQRG ZGCIGGQ CIU TGUTAG.

—NKRCUV ZUVFG

112 T represents W

113 O represents P

114 D represents S

112

It is a damned poor mind indeed that can't think of at least two ways of spelling any word.

—Andrew Jackson

113

Absences are a good influence in love and help keep it bright and delicate.

—Robert Louis Stevenson

114

Laughter is the shortest distance between two people.

—Victor Borge

115

Z WZQ ODGHDR HJ SHPD WZPHFN Z IZPD RHXV ZSS XVD WDJX HFNODQHDFXJ ZFQ VZGHFN JMLDMFD JHX MF HX.

—QZFHDSSD JXDDS

116

JVX DXEJ GLHP LE VX CVZ BHOXE JVX EBHGGXEJ HBZTQJ ZR GFLQW WZ JVX GZQWXEJ CHF.

—EHBTXG DTJGXP

117

W ARHZE VSALPSG WF WEJZU YRSF RS TSWZHOSG URWU RS RWG W THKRU FLU LFZQ UL VS THKRU VJU WZGL UL VS YTLFK.

—URLPWG GOWGO

115 W represents B
116 G represents L
117 F represents N

115

A bad review is like baking a cake with all the best ingredients and having someone sit on it.

—Danielle Steel

116

The best liar is he who makes the smallest amount of lying go the longest way.

—Samuel Butler

117

A child becomes an adult when he realizes that he has a right not only to be right but also to be wrong.

—Thomas Szasz

118

SZKMKSQTM SGARHRQR GE PZKQ LGV CG GA QZT QZHMC KAC EGVMQZ QMHTR.

—NKUTR UHSZTATM

119

TXKFRR LZT YEZZRF NZ CZ WJFHN NEGXWR VGNE GN, GN UHQFR XZ CGSSFJFXYF EZV UTYE MZVFJ LZT EHPF.

—ZMJHE VGXSJFL

120

IT S NOT A GOOD IDEA TO TRY TO PUT YOUR
NZ'W OXZ G UXXJ NJQG ZX ZMV ZX LFZ VXFM
WIFE INTO A NOVEL NOT YOUR LATEST
DNYQ NOZX G OXSQR . . . OXZ VXFM RGZQWZ
WIFE ANYWAY
DNYQ GOVDGV.

NORMAN MAILER
—OXMBGO BGNRQM

118 R represents S | 119 X represents N | 120 V represents Y

118

Character consists of what you do on the third and fourth tries.

—James Michener

119

Unless you choose to do great things with it, it makes no difference how much power you have.

—Oprah Winfrey

120

It's not a good idea to try to put your wife into a novel . . . not your latest wife anyway.

—Norman Mailer

121

XNO VPCJOL SVO HFAX FJSPX XNO VODE COBQF QE XNFX XNOG YSKO HQWNXE. DNOV GSP WQKO XNOC ASVHLSVXFXQSVE GSP WOX FXXOVXQSV.

—VODX WQVWLQAN

122

BTRVXIN XR Z KZIWXLN VWZV, DWNL RPKNPLN WZR PLIN QXUNL XV VWN RVZGVXLQ YTRW, GPCCR PL PM XVRNCM.

—BPWL QZCRDPGVWA

123

DBQ WYQFDQID WXXP ZXK TFM PX GXY FMXDBQY HI MXD NKID DX IBFYQ ZXKY YHTBQI AKD DX YQCQFO DX BHS BHI XEM.

—AQMNFSHM PHIYFQOH

121 G represents Y

122 X represents I

123 W represents G

121

The number one fact about the news media is that they love fights. When you give them confrontations you get attention.

—Newt Gingrich

122

Justice is a machine that, when someone has once given it the starting push, rolls on of itself.

—John Galsworthy

123

The greatest good you can do for another is not just to share your riches but to reveal to him his own.

—Benjamin Disraeli

124

JCVS IGX UBD LGT ZVTLVRNBGS, IGX FBWRGHVT BN'W U DGHBSA NUTAVN.

—AVGTAV LBWCVT

125

GSIIXZJEE XE FXWJ S YVBBJQAFL KGXNG SIIJSQE SZP PJFXRGBE VE ADQ DZJ YQXJA UDUJZB, YVB EDDZ AFXBE SKSL.

—SZZS ISMFDMS

126

QAYRS SDE QHDYAXH GUJ MXUDC UAX GUXRNUEY DXH. QZ QREC JDEIY IU YHH IU REBRERIZ.

—YIHFRH JUECHX

124 S represents N

125 K represents W

126 Y represents S

124

When you aim for perfection, you discover it's a moving target.

—George Fisher

125

Happiness is like a butterfly which appears and delights us for one brief moment, but soon flits away.

—Anna Pavlova

126

Music can measure how broad our horizons are. My mind wants to see to infinity.

—Stevie Wonder

127

UQ OG HZZIC AWP HRRS WSG XZJCR U XZFDP SZM AWTR HRRS USTUMRP MZ AZDDGXZZP, WSP UQ MARG AWP HRRS WSG HRMMRJ U XZFDP SZM AWTR EZOR.

—JWGOZSP EAWSPDRJ

128

EUWOOTQL CG WUU QCAYO–CE LMJ SMD'O CDYWUT.

—WSUWC GOTRTDGMD

129

NGZSTFTA NHQTL KH SGTV QCXS KH SNBET ZX NTYY ZX QTL SH RT SGHCIGS GZYJ ZX IHHK. YCEUBYV, SGBX BX LHS KBJJBECYS.

—EGZAYHSST NGBSSHL

127 M represents T

128 E represents F

129 N represents W

127

If my books had been any worse I would not have been invited to Hollywood, and if they had been any better I would not have come.

—Raymond Chandler

128

Flattery is all right—if you don't inhale.

—Adlai Stevenson

129

Whatever women do they must do twice as well as men to be thought half as good. Luckily, this is not difficult.

—Charlotte Whitton

130

LNU GFJXXYNXYGJIV IN TJPP ILGE XPJFVI VJYIL ULVF TPVJYPH GI GE NTVJF.

—JYILRY T. TPJYZV

131

QEY WBXF QESBT QEUQ VQWDV TWO HJWN VYBOSBT UBWQEYJ HXWWO SV QEUQ QEY HSJVQ WBY CUV GVYXYVV.

—BSKEWXUV KEUNHWJQ

132

BZD LYE GOWLZRUT VZTU YSZDQ Y XUTWZE OE YE NZDT ZC XJYB QNYE OE Y BUYT ZC LZERUTWYQOZE.

—XJYQZ

130 F represents N

131 V represents S

132 B represents Y

130

How inappropriate to call this planet Earth when clearly it is Ocean.

—Arthur C. Clarke

131

The only thing that stops God from sending another flood is that the first one was useless.

—Nicholas Chamfort

132

You can discover more about a person in an hour of play than in a year of conversation.

—Plato

133

IUDF'C AMH J LJIRUGK CEJNBL, J WBBQ WIJTFQ HEJH CHQMHC JGN DQFHC EUC EBMQ MWBG HEF CHJKF, JGN HEFG UC EFJQN GB YBQF.

—LUIIUJY CEJRFCWFJQF

134

CNBUM BD MZP IQBWP SP IJX SBUUBTCUX HLQ KLBTC SZJM SP JQP CLBTC ML KL JTXSJX.

—BDJEPUUP ZLUUJTK

135

R JRCKX JF FNK AOTIRB'M NKJYF, JGX TD JBBRXKGF R NRF RF RG FNK MFHCJBN.

—OAFHG MRGBIJRY

133 G represents N

134 S represents W

135 B represents C

133

Life's but a walking shadow, a poor player that struts and frets his hour upon the stage, and then is heard no more.

—William Shakespeare

134

Guilt is the price we pay willingly for doing what we are going to do anyway.

—Isabelle Holland

135

I aimed at the public's heart, and by accident I hit it in the stomach.

—Upton Sinclair

136

VFY ZESZHPY GDK Z JDDA LFDRWE JY ZV WYZLV ZL IRPF ZL VFY PDLV DG VFY WRHPF ZV QFCPF CV QZL ECLPRLLYE.

—PZWSCH VKCWWCH

137

RY R UKMJ "DRBMJAJGGK," EFJ KSMRJBDJ CNSGM QJ GNNZRBH NSE YNA K QNMV RB EFJ DNKDF.

—KGYAJM FREDFDNDZ

138

TIVNBQNPXY, KXCI TPUQXOW, NPBGKA DILXV UO PBSI; DGO, GVKXCI TPUQXOW, XO NPBGKA IVA OPIQI.

—TKUQI DBBOPI KGTI

136 F represents H — 137 N represents O — 138 D represents B

136

The advance for a book should be at least as much as the cost of the lunch at which it was discussed.

—Calvin Trillin

137

If I made "Cinderella," the audience would be looking out for a body in the coach.

—Alfred Hitchcock

138

Censorship, like charity, should begin at home; but, unlike charity, it should end there.

—Clare Boothe Luce

139

ZJYTBSG, VUTW JS YTPJWX SE SCFT BEES, JX C OZCWS EA BCOJI PBEVSU.

—PTEBPT VCXUJWPSEW

140

ZX VBP CORU CBMJ CKGG LBRK, EKGKTU O DPEV NOR; UIK BUIKM JZRL IOE RB UZNK.

—KGDKMU IPDDOML

141

GBUBT VGKYHQ WG WHHVJWQNT YGQVH WOQBT INY RWUB XTNKKBP QRB TVUBT.

—XNTPBHH RYHH

139 B represents R

140 R represents N

141 W represents A

139

Liberty, when it begins to take root, is a plant of rapid growth.

—George Washington

140

If you want work well done, select a busy man; the other kind has no time.

—Elbert Hubbard

141

Never insult an alligator until after you have crossed the river.

—Cordell Hull

142

ZOCTS SQB HCXS CUEFEJZNESL SQZS ZJL MUESBU DZJ QCIB SC ZDQEBPB QCJBXSNL EX SC XSBZN MESQ FCCY RTYFHBJS.

—RCXQ OENNEJFX

143

FPZA ZD ZHAPCJ WGYQO AC FJGAQ NCOA GO PGO OGBDZAHJQ CD APQ XZTY CU Z TPQTY.

—XJQDIZD UJZDTGO

144

N PGWCP VJSICGS N ZYT SC HSNDK CD VJZZ TYS NPCGDK HCWY CSIYP VNA.

—QCID SGKCP

142 F represents G 143 Y represents K 144 V represents W

142

About the most originality that any writer can hope to achieve honestly is to steal with good judgment.

—Josh Billings

143

What an author likes to write most is his signature on the back of a check.

—Brendan Francis

144

A rumor without a leg to stand on will get around some other way.

—John Tudor

145

RDHTL LHXDT LZZM CNPDSHNJ HA JHFD
RDHTL NAAHLTDM PZ RNFD N YNFD NTM
UNXHTL PUD RNPPDS CNMD WZS GZQ.

—SZANJHTM SQAADJJ

146

KMS'Y DMSKGFDGSK YM ESFXHIIGK IZUMB.
YBQ HY VMB JZIV Z KZQ VHBFY.

—UBMMXF ZYXHSFMS

147

PA MFQ XEHPR PAIEHMJN B ZQVQAI PH
EHEBZZN AL XLJQ MFBA HLXQLAQ DPMF MDL
RLAHQREMPCQ FPM HPAVZQH.

—VBJJN MJEIQBE

145 L represents G

146 B represents R

147 Z represents L

145

Being given good material is like being assigned to bake a cake and having the batter made for you.

—Rosalind Russell

146

Don't condescend to unskilled labor. Try it for half a day first.

—Brooks Atkinson

147

In the music industry a legend is usually no more than someone with two consecutive hit singles.

—Garry Trudeau

148

DOGS COME WHEN THEY'RE CALLED CATS
NVCM BVKW ILWT SLWJ'FW BZDDWN; BZSM
TAKE A MESSAGE AND GET BACK TO YOU
SZYW Z KWMMZCW ZTN CWS XZBY SV JVQ.

MARY BLY
—KZFJ XDJ

149

JBOXGZVET VR G IQENQJRRVHJ BVRXEHJQU EC EOQ EPT VNTEQGTXJ.

—PVMM BOQGTZ

150

XA PCOR GTCI OSQ SYQ TVVCHRQGTQA GDR PTVMRI MS KS GSXRUZTFR GDR'I VRHRQ JRRV JROSQR. C GTCI, "DSP 'JSYM MDR NCMFDRV?"

—QSIVRA ITVKRQOCRZI

148 M represents S · 149 B represents D · 150 G represents S

148

Dogs come when they're called; cats take a message and get back to you.

—Mary Bly

149

Education is a progressive discovery of our own ignorance.

—Will Durant

150

My wife said for our anniversary she wanted to go someplace she'd never been before. I said, "How 'bout the kitchen?"

—Rodney Dangerfield

151

KQENGUX WNZRV GNVIMRVQEQKQUX. UBZU QV HBX WMVU WNR AGNZA QU.

—JNMGJN ENGRZGA VBZH

152

XDR JRLGFI TJLIBULJRIXG LIB TJLIBVDAWBJRI TRX LWFIT GF PRWW AG XDLX XDRZ DLYR L VFOOFI RIROZ.

—GLO WRYRIGFI

153

KGZMCU SKL QPMSMQO WPGMOL INH MO XMJL KGZMCU SKL KGCUFGC OGI INH'ZL UNS G WPLSSI CLQJ.

—LXM AGXXGQK

151 Q represents I

152 T represents G

153 C represents N

151

Liberty means responsibility. That is why most men dread it.

—George Bernard Shaw

152

The reason grandparents and grandchildren get along so well is that they have a common enemy.

—Sam Levenson

153

Having the critics praise you is like having the hangman say you've got a pretty neck.

—Eli Wallach

154

U AZQYK RMVDQCM DZ FQMBB DIOD OVZV, AIZ ACZDM BZ GOVX JZMGB AUDIZQD BUFVUVF DIMG, AOB ZLDMV O AZGOV.

—RUCFUVUO AZZYL

155

HGKQWCWJ K DKT ZJKSB XNJ, GW ZJKSB XNJ K DOJKFEW. WCWJS ZJKSWJ JWUPFWB OQBWEX QN QGOB: "LJWKQ LNU, LJKTQ QGKQ QHOFW QHN AW TNQ XNPJ."

—OCKT QPJLWTWC

156

PCUQ KL RYTUH LY EYSUKFQ EYYJ, LCU XUHH IGLCUQLKR LCU MULLUS.

—FUSIXJ QIRCTIQ

154 F represents G

155 J represents R

156 X represents L

154

I would venture to guess that Anon, who wrote so many poems without signing them, was often a woman.

—Virginia Woolf

155

Whatever a man prays for, he prays for a miracle. Every prayer reduces itself to this: "Great God, grant that twice two be not four."

—Ivan Turgenev

156

When it comes to foreign food, the less authentic the better.

—Gerald Nachman

157

IZLOTPQFZC FC QOIHOT FB PMVPXB P UFTQEO, GEQ IZLOTPQFZC FC HTFCJFHMO FB PMVPXB P UFJO.

—QKZIPB HPFCO

158

APJI ISTWRHZN OZ LN QTI IPJI OTGLZ NIJSN SWQ CTS TCCLVZ, RWI IPJI IPZE CLQX LI ZJNE IT BZI ZHZVIZX.

—NPJQJ JHZKJQXZS

159

SY SL YEI ZGWGFD CU CRB GXI YEGY YEI DCRHX GBI LC NRLD YIGKESHX RL YEGY YEID EGPI HC YSZI WIUY YC WIGBH.

—IBSK ECUUIB

157 Z represents O
158 Q represents N
159 X represents G

157

Moderation in temper is always a virtue, but moderation in principle is always a vice.

—Thomas Paine

158

What troubles me is not that movie stars run for office, but that they find it easy to get elected.

—Shana Alexander

159

It is the malady of our age that the young are so busy teaching us that they have no time left to learn.

—Eric Hoffer

160

JEK TGBRI OBR TOYKI OFK OPTOMI QB JEK IGRK QH JEK OUPKIJ BOYGWOJQFI.

—KRTOFR WGUUQB

161

Z MNNX NCVDQ QN MI ZB SOI FSOX QN MLIZX CF QDI JLNGIB HIZ RSQDSB CH.

—JLZBG XZJXZ

162

CRFJEZWF EUW JGW AFAEP XURITW XWJKWWM WLOWURWMVW EMI KRFINC.

—OGQPPRF JGWUNAL

160 O represents A   161 M represents B   162 F represents S

160

The winds and waves are always on the side of the ablest navigators.

—Edward Gibbon

161

A book ought to be an ice pick to break up the frozen sea within us.

—Franz Kafka

162

Mistakes are the usual bridge between experience and wisdom.

—Phyllis Theroux

163

JQNNXMOWW XW COMOSXTXQP SUI VJO CUAL, CBV XV XW YIXOS VJQV AOFOPUNW VJO NUROIW US VJO ZXMA.

—ZQITOP NIUBWV

164

JAAZ TAPPBHGTUEGAH GV UV VEGPBMUEGHJ UV LMUTO TASSCC, UHZ FBVE UV DUIZ EA VMCCY USECI.

—UHHC PAIIAR MGHZLCIJD

165

VJFZMH ZV J VRMF RE LAJVV, NBHMHZX KHBRACHMV CR LHXHMJAAT CZVYRIHM HIHMTKRCT'V EJYH KQF FBHZM RNX.

—DRXJFBJX VNZEF

163 U represents O | 164 G represents I | 165 H represents E

163

Happiness is beneficial for the body, but it is grief that develops the powers of the mind.

—Marcel Proust

164

Good communication is as stimulating as black coffee, and just as hard to sleep after.

—Anne Morrow Lindbergh

165

Satire is a sort of glass, wherein beholders do generally discover everybody's face but their own.

—Jonathan Swift

166

HJNDN LG GX PQUJ KQLSCQA LM PI XRNM HJNDN LG XMSI DXXP HX KZVN Z GLMOSN UQAUZVN.

—AJISSLG CLSSND

167

TGEDPDL AGNOVR QZLLNZFD NR Z INIAJ INIAJ BLEBERNANEO MEDRO'A VOET AGD GZCI EI NA.

—ILZOVCNO B. SEODR

168

QR EUS PDMN NU VDZX IXDSNQRSJ VSYQL, EUS VSYN KJDE NAX IJDLZ DMC NAX PAQNX MUNXY NUWXNAXH.

—HQLADHC MQFUM

166 P represents M   167 L represents R   168 E represents Y

166

There is so much buildup in my oven there is only room to bake a single cupcake.

—Phyllis Diller

167

Whoever thinks marriage is a fifty-fifty proposition doesn't know the half of it.

—Franklin P. Jones

168

If you want to make beautiful music, you must play the black and the white notes together.

—Richard Nixon

169

G ZXPL SH GCH XRTLZ CGWL IXVJE PWLJJ GP PILLR, SVR IXVJE CXR BXPR TGJD GP WVBT EVZNCF RTL INCRLZ WXCRTP.

—FLXZFL GEL

170

T AFEI F SFN KAFK T SFXX LXFKKINP CISFRZI TK BIKZ QI MHVAINI.

—AIMMP PHRMBQFM

171

GOD GAVE US OURMEMORIES SO THAT WE
JCQ JZMY FA CFI XYXCIEYA AC LKZL UY
MIGHT HAVEROSES IN DECEMBER
XEJKL KZMY ICAYA ES QYPYXDYI.

JAMES M BARRIE
—VZXYA X. DZIIEY

169 P represents S

170 S represents C

171 A represents S

169

A rose by any other name would smell as sweet, but would not cost half as much during the winter months.

—George Ade

170

I have a car that I call Flattery because it gets me nowhere.

—Henny Youngman

171

God gave us our memories so that we might have roses in December.

—James M. Barrie

172

QLD QDXQ EYJ NLDQLDJ YJ PYQ KYT GHP LYWZ H IYC XLYTWZ PYQ CD QLD HJJHPMDRDPQ YE KYTJ GLJYRYXYRDX.

—CDWWH HCATM

173

ULF LFA ICULF LPV KIC DCBEVA BLZEVKZ, CX INSBN VLBN BCFKLSFZ KNV EVQ KC KNV CKNVP.

—SZLE ASFVZVF

174

GCTGWAWEHW RL FZJ WCF TN GJCLVWHREA TFZJCL TN MZWF DTV HTE'F SJBRJOJ DTVCLJBN.

—WSSW JSWE

172 T represents U 173 F represents N 174 D represents Y

172

The test for whether or not you can hold a job should not be the arrangement of your chromosomes.

—Bella Abzug

173

Man and woman are two locked caskets, of which each contains the key to the other.

—Isak Dinesen

174

Propaganda is the art of persuading others of what you don't believe yourself.

—Abba Eban

175

XOOXEJCPBJBLY QEL XSJLP JIBPUY TXC IQDLP'J PXJBMLW JIL SBEYJ JBNL QEXCPW.

—MQJILEBPL WLPLCDL

176

GM HTO RLFE ET VGYY LFH GBJL GF EIJ RTNYB ETBLH, SJE L XTQQGEEJJ RTNVGFS TF GE.

—XILNYJW M. VJEEJNGFS

177

KEPX ZWO W KFU OEJCKXQ ZBXA ZBWU ZX BFAFQXT ZWO PWUBXQ WAT JFUBXQ QWUBXQ UBWA WKK JWIFQ VQXTEU VWQTO.

—QFRXQU FQRXA

175 I represents H

176 B represents D

177 Z represents W

175

Opportunities are often things you haven't noticed the first time around.

—Catherine Deneuve

176

If you want to kill any idea in the world today, get a committee working on it.

—Charles F. Kettering

177

Life was a lot simpler when what we honored was father and mother rather than all major credit cards.

—Robert Orben

178

NLJJWO WJ JLXYVQWIN VQTV IL LIY EBTWXJ VL BWAY-GZV YSYCMGLUM YIRLMJ.

—RLJYOQ ELICTU

179

BQH'R VQRE SR VM BQEJ MK ZSBRJNK Q XMTE MK QTV.

—ZJHTL BSNNJT

180

OSRYBFJLD YH BAD VCEG OVVP PRSJKED DCVRXA BV KDFVND J OJNYEG ADYSEVVN.

—SRHHDEE KJLDS

178 I represents N

179 E represents K

180 B represents T

178

Gossip is something that no one claims to like—but everybody enjoys.

—Joseph Conrad

179

Man's task is to make of himself a work of art.

—Henry Miller

180

Fruitcake is the only food durable enough to become a family heirloom.

—Russell Baker

181

VNJJD, OCBUJV, MYA UJMNHU GZVH EJ CYHJOOZDHJA HQ EJ HOZNR JYSQRJA.

—SJMY DMZN OCBUHJO

182

PRFE XFHLMTZW. VFR'Y DBBTQY XFHL VFS'M DVGNLDYNFR DM BFRBZHMNJT TJNVTRBT YKDY XFH DLT EFRVTLWHZ.

—DRR ZDRVTLM

183

JLXUZELXUHNZUG ZJ QXNG JLXUZELXU UPHU MSOJ GQS UPL TMQXR THG.

—T. JQELMJLU EHSRPHE

181 D represents P

182 J represents V

183 G represents Y

181

Sleep, riches, and health must be interrupted to be truly enjoyed.

—Jean Paul Richter

182

Know yourself. Don't accept your dog's admiration as conclusive evidence that you are wonderful.

—Ann Landers

183

Sentimentality is only sentiment that rubs you the wrong way.

—W. Somerset Maugham

184

ZGPCMLIARQ ILCVKID UGMRARNR AM RLDAMV "IGCO ZGMKR AR OKLO" NG YKGYIK XFG MKJKC BMKX IGCO ZGMKR XLR LIAJK.

—V.B. UFKRNKCNGM

185

TH GQPNBL SQV LCDOBZ DO PNB FLQVN. Q VPEFMKLEMBL XCTIBZ ECP EG Q SDOZES QOZ GBAA EO NDV ICVNFQLP.

—XQFMDB TQVEO

186

PYZ QM P GQYG KNQDZ ES KPX ISN RPETNQEX.

—ESR MESKKPNU

184 R represents S

185 B represents E

186 Y represents G

184

Journalism largely consists in saying "Lord Jones is dead" to people who never knew Lord Jones was alive.

—G.K. Chesterton

185

My father was ruined in the crash. A stockbroker jumped out of a window and fell on his pushcart.

—Jackie Mason

186

Age is a high price to pay for maturity.

—Tom Stoppard

187

W TU PBCH EZAK ZE SCXSQ, NXS AZS TS TYY ZE UTCSHCKZU.

—PZYSTWCB

188

PN DT RXEEIZ SGZ XE TEK ZI IGL KPNNTLTERTW, XZ MTXWZ DT RXE UTMS VXOT ZUT DILMK WXNT NIL KPBTLWPZF.

—QIUE N. OTEETKF

189

HWBV, EOQLWK UQHYLNLDLHW, L GZA RHQBVE DH JLIV RHQ EZTA HW WHDYLWK NOD RHHE ZWE GZDVQ.

—G.B. RLVJEA

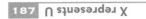

187 X represents U 188 D represents W 189 W represents N

187

I am very fond of truth, but not at all of martyrdom.

—Voltaire

188

If we cannot put an end to our differences, at least we can help make the world safe for diversity.

—John F. Kennedy

189

Once, during Prohibition, I was forced to live for days on nothing but food and water.

—W.C. Fields

190

LKCP LSXCP VS LOSPV, XCP VS OHVKJ GRJCO JKCX.

—XGC LCTJ

191

RQEBDXC ZL FCZJX LRDBCP SQ PCDSO—DJP LDPPNZJX EH DJVGDV.

—YQOJ GDVJC

192

Z FTJG TECGTPD LZJGI UAW MWYBZIB UW UFG ATC TIP Z BUTIP CGTPD UW BTMCZQZMG SD AZQG'B VCWUFGC.

—TCUGSYB ATCP

190 V represents G

191 X represents G

192 U represents T

190

When women go wrong, men go right after them.

—Mae West

191

Courage is being scared to death—and saddling up anyway.

—John Wayne

192

I have already given two cousins to the war and I stand ready to sacrifice my wife's brother.

—Artemus Ward

193

WMP NOUR OFF VNR ENOAOEVRALXVLEX MK O DMDPFOA DMFLVLELOG: O NMAALTFR UMLER, TOH TARRHLGZ, OGH O UPFZOA JOGGRA.

—OALXVMDNOGRX

194

SH SNEC VM GJWQ DNX OQWMC INK WMC BWKHIXE GJWQ DNX IWEE INK.

—KXQJ SNNKOQVM

195

JI BRSSO JBSIRFB JBA SCWA LMT YLKK IY L YCMA, YRKK WAMJAMQA CW KCPA TAYOCMF JBA SIKA IY JCZA CM BRZLM KCYA.

—PAMMAJB QKLSP

193 L represents I | 194 I represents F | 195 Y represents F

193

You have all the characteristics of a popular politician: a horrible voice, bad breeding, and a vulgar manner.

—Aristophanes

194

Be bold in what you stand for and careful what you fall for.

—Ruth Boorstin

195

To hurry through the rise and fall of a fine, full sentence is like defying the role of time in human life.

—Kenneth Clark

196

JTTNLZYB CUBLV JTJLNLB; TNLZYB CUBLV VLBND.

—L.V. BDJUL

197

XKQGT'V LNIGXIVX EGSKN-VGJWAL QIJWZI WV XKUKNNKF.

—XKU FWEVKA

198

SEC UIPPCUUXIK ZCLVKISDVRJZF DU J USJSCUHJR, SEC IRUIPPCUUXIK VRC J PZDHDRJK.

—CZDPE XZVHH

196 T represents M

197 I represents E

198 I represents U

196

Immature poets imitate; mature poets steal.

—T.S. Eliot

197

Today's greatest labor-saving device is tomorrow.

—Tom Wilson

198

The successful revolutionary is a statesman, the unsuccessful one a criminal.

—Erich Fromm

199

BDHMHKV HI PGIN. GFF NAO JA HI IMGDP GM G QFGKW ILPPM AS TGTPD OKMHF JDATI AS QFAAJ SADX AK NAOD SADPLPGJ.

—VPKP SABFPD

200

LKWFH MNEGWTTHS MECWO WA AXWT ON OXAOH ALHHOHE, WO CACXFFI AZNWFA MXAOHE.

—XGWVXWF YXS GCEHS

201

QZJ QFPEYA HCLMFYV ZEHV YZ YGZAM XGZ HZDM CY, PEJ PFM PHXPVA FMPJV YZ QIPFJ PEJ JMOMEJ CY.

—JPECMH XMLAYMF

199 N represents Y 200 O represents T 201 J represents D

199

Writing is easy. All you do is stare at a blank sheet of paper until drops of blood form on your forehead.

—Gene Fowler

200

While forbidden fruit is said to taste sweeter, it usually spoils faster.

—Abigail Van Buren

201

God grants liberty only to those who love it, and are always ready to guard and defend it.

—Daniel Webster

202

IATV, ISFV OVCJHLOHRJ MHCM AO PMSPFVR CHIHN, GLCJ EV JHFVR ZSJM EISRN DHSJM AO SJ IACVC SJC DIHTAO.

—MVIVR OAZIHRN

203

SU TUYSQTXU XB SWDTNQ FSU HN WNQTQONV, HKO UXO SU TVNS IGXQN OTDN GSQ FXDN.

—YTFOXW GKZX

204

OAH UWQH AH OMCNHI WK AXV AWBWQ OAH KMVOHQ PH DWGBOHI WGQ VEWWBV.

—QMCEA PMCIW HUHQVWB

202 I represents L

203 H represents B

204 A represents H

202

Love, like restaurant hash or chicken salad, must be taken with blind faith or it loses its flavor.

—Helen Rowland

203

An invasion of armies can be resisted, but not an idea whose time has come.

—Victor Hugo

204

The more he talked of his honor the faster we counted our spoons.

—Ralph Waldo Emerson

205

DXRT EX OBQ MOQB QXEUQRQMBO; M HRO AMOT QSX GRC ECYXDA.

—KMQR ERX LKBGO

206

ERHX XAOANT IJAKXN TAK PHHFP LA FHIPKJH KQ, GL'P LGFH LA VRHVS TAKJ TIJNPLGVS.

—OGCC CHFCHT

207

HIJ OHKUJ SMZGM UHFTB GKTNZU CWK UMT KHZI YABU IWU RT BAKOKZBTN ZC ZUB WOOWITIUB RXHYT ZU CWK UMT NKWALMU.

—NSZLMU S. YWKKWS

205 X represents E 206 K represents U 207 M represents H

205

Lead me not into temptation; I can find the way myself.

—Rita Mae Brown

206

When nobody around you seems to measure up, it's time to check your yardstick.

—Bill Lemley

207

Any party which takes credit for the rain must not be surprised if its opponents blame it for the drought.

—Dwight W. Morrow

208

YFW PCJBW XR AXYFXM HCG. PCJBW HCGJRWVP.

—FSJJXRCM PCJO

209

S FNLVWRDBNJ BD S YBUYZTNX EPTL QNT S EPLVESEBNJ XP'TP JNE ETKBJU ENN YSTC EN TPDBDE.

—YWUY SRRPJ

210

YF OCI QVOVSI IRISXPFI HYKK EI HPSKW-QULPVD QPS QYQOIIF LYFVOID.

—UFWX HUSCPK

208 P represents F

209 Y represents H

210 I represents E

208

The force is within you. Force yourself.

—Harrison Ford

209

A compulsion is a highbrow term for a temptation we're not trying too hard to resist.

—Hugh Allen

210

In the future everyone will be world-famous for fifteen minutes.

—Andy Warhol

211

DAMJS OAM OCHDS FYSNCYZ ANXS CSNISCJ; DAMJS OAM OCHDS MVJFECSYZ ANXS FMRRSQDNDMCJ.

—NYVSCD FNREJ

212

SJLYSDALSA DY X HJNZAU-DL-BXO OZJYA KDYDN LAKAU ALGY.

—Z.B. HALSTAL

213

QCY VHNPQ CGFV MV MTN FHBYP HP NTHAYS RI MTN OGNYAQP GAS QCY PYXMAS CGFV RI MTN XCHFSNYA.

—XFGNYAXY SGNNMK

211 O represents W   212 K represents V   213 V represents F

211

Those who write clearly have readers; those who write obscurely have commentators.

—Albert Camus

212

Conscience is a mother-in-law whose visit never ends.

—H.L. Mencken

213

The first half of our lives is ruined by our parents and the second half by our children.

—Clarence Darrow

214

RFCJS FNL BLFQHWE YG MFR EJVYMT EYLJPHWG, QNR EJMJTYMT RUWE.

—HSMCFM ZFUMGFM

215

UVL BFV ZIFEDWEWVQ NZUIDNBFVNSWZ WN CFI HLDDLI DSFV CWCDR ZILFESWVQ WD.

—XVKDL IUEXVL

216

CGXHLN NGEKAZ DQ UJZQ JN NXUBAQ JN BENNXDAQ, DKC HEC JHF NXUBAQP.

—JADQPC QXHNCQXH

214 T represents G

215 C represents F

216 N represents S

214

Today our problem is not making miracles, but managing them.

—Lyndon Johnson

215

One man practicing sportsmanship is far better than fifty preaching it.

—Knute Rockne

216

Things should be made as simple as possible, but not any simpler.

—Albert Einstein

217

QZHE EZUG PIXAEBL ADDFG UG NIBD XADNSJILDF SIJUEUPUHAG.

—DFQHBF JHAKJDL

218

VGC EIH CPLCE GU GC; VGHDZPIZJGUM GH HGFYSB ZISGHCEDUGZH VGCE VRPAH.

—ARPRCEB YIPJDP

219

RPEAZPA FDZARKRVZARQP AZJME AQQ HQPF.

—VZDDRM KRETMD

217 G represents S

218 E represents H

219 P represents N

217

What this country needs is more unemployed politicians.

—Edward Langley

218

Wit has truth in it; wisecracking is simply calisthenics with words.

—Dorothy Parker

219

Instant gratification takes too long.

—Carrie Fisher

220

GKDCPIYM KFUY RHIY MYYP HQ RHPYCL SKFM HQ GIDSDGL.

—GFIHCNM GHFSL

221

CRSJVYJLJ, CRSJMYZDT ZDFLJGZUWJ ZC VHZMZDT MR UJ NDRVD.

—FHLW CHTHD

222

LPQMEMCQZR, FSYZ YZUIEKYT PXQZ MSY JYJQID, UCKY DQP UQQT MSQPUSMR.

—FCZRMQZ OSPIOSCWW

220 M represents N

221 J represents E

222 S represents H

220

Children have more need of models than of critics.

—Carolyn Coats

221

Somewhere, something incredible is waiting to be known.

—Carl Sagan

222

Quotations, when engraved upon the memory, give you good thoughts.

—Winston Churchill

223

T AKNB EAB ZBLSBHE GTVZFTSTBW EKO SMLV SML EAB QMNBLCVBCE. JAI WMC'E EABI UPGE ZLTCE MPL VMCBI JTEA K LBEPLC KWWLBGG MC TE?

—DMD AMZB

224

PET ZRWTUPWJWR PETIHA W VWYT NTZP WZ PEFP PET HWUOZ IJ ZFPSHU FHT RIGLIZTK TUPWHTVA IJ VIZP FWHVWUT VSOOFOT.

—GFHY HSZZTVV

225

OVH OTJYRBH SPOV GJUUPIU PN OVWO, RX OVH OPEH XJY THWBPQH XJY'TH IJO PI NVWMH DJT PO, PO'N OJJ DWT OJ SWBF RWLF.

—DTWIFBPI M. GJIHN

223 Z represents P | 224 V represents L | 225 I represents N

223

I have the perfect simplified tax form for the government. Why don't they just print our money with a return address on it?

—Bob Hope

224

The scientific theory I like best is that the rings of Saturn are composed entirely of lost airline luggage.

—Mark Russell

225

The trouble with jogging is that, by the time you realize you're not in shape for it, it's too far to walk back.

—Franklin P. Jones

226

RMEVPGJP VD DHNPEAVGW UHT MONVZP VG EAP OZVKPZ CPAVGO UHT, MGO DJHZG VG EAP HGP MAPMO.

—NMJ NJJFPMZU

227

PRLX DJJLBCFERAJ DXN PRLX KEAQRKJ RA FGN KRXWQ. JVXLO FGNB RSS NTNXP RAVN EA D KGEWN, RX FGN WEYGF KRA'F VRBN EA.

—DWDA DWQD

228

BOIM QEM QGLO YXLI BOXYNQ EVPGB TIPTHI EB BOIXA JGYIAEHQ BOEB XB RESIQ RI QEW BOEB X'R NPXYN BP RXQQ RXYI VM KGQB E JIF WEMQ.

—NEAAXQPY SIXHHPA

226 O represents D | 227 K represents W | 228 G represents U

226

Patience is something you admire in the driver behind you, and scorn in the one ahead.

—Mac McCleary

227

Your assumptions are your windows on the world. Scrub them off every once in a while, or the light won't come in.

—Alan Alda

228

They say such nice things about people at their funerals that it makes me sad that I'm going to miss mine by just a few days.

—Garrison Keillor

229

TB'P YUYCTJM BIYB BIO YUAKJB AH JOEP BIYB IYVVOJP TJ BIO EAWZX ONOWD XYD YZEYDP FKPB OLYSBZD HTBP BIO JOEPVYYVOW.

—FOWWD POTJHOZX

230

EUJ'P OJUNO PCQ DQZPCQH; JKJQ-PQJPCI UM PCQ XQUXRQ NUFREJ'P IPZHP Z NUJWQHIZPKUJ KM KP EKEJ'P NCZJYQ UJNQ KJ Z DCKRQ.

—OKJ CFAAZHE

231

STFLJIY NUAO TYG FUODYOC RYL JTLU S KSX LURYLZYO GJLZUAL SORAJTR, S XSTD OUXXYOF ZSC WACL LSDYT VMSKY.

—WUZTTF KSOCUT

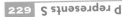

229 P represents S   230 C represents H   231 X represents B

229

It's amazing that the amount of news that happens in the world every day always just exactly fits the newspaper.

—Jerry Seinfeld

230

Don't knock the weather; nine-tenths of the people couldn't start a conversation if it didn't change once in a while.

—Kin Hubbard

231

Anytime four New Yorkers get into a cab together without arguing, a bank robbery has just taken place.

—Johnny Carson

232

DU WNMUMIGKC GK DU WYJWQC BPM BGZZ XUMB CMIMQQMB BPL CPW CPGUFK PW JQWHGNCWH LWKCWQHDL HGHU'C PDJJWU.

—WDQZ BGZKMU

233

BRXMV FMQYZ JY XPM VJBN KJ IOAP Q UBYX XJ KWMYN IJVM XQIM UQXP IE RBIQDE, UPJ Q PMBV BVM UJYNMVROD WMJWDM.

—PJUQM IBYNMD

234

NJD HMG IJC VR RPSRHARK AJ YJERTG M HJCGATI ANMA NML ADJ NCGKTRK MGK BJTAI-LXP QXGKL JB HNRRLR?

—HNMTORL KR YMCOOR

232 G represents I

233 U represents W

234 H represents C

232

An economist is an expert who will know tomorrow why the things he predicted yesterday didn't happen.

—Earl Wilson

233

After being on the road so much I want to spend more time with my family, who I hear are wonderful people.

—Howie Mandel

234

How can you be expected to govern a country that has two hundred and forty-six kinds of cheese?

—Charles de Gaulle

235

ATCI TX ATJI H G-QWMTI. ZWE LWK'V NHKV VW AIHMI TK VPI QTLLAI WC TV, GEV ZWE LWK'V NHKV VW XII TV HOHTK.

—VIL VEUKIU

236

GA GAPA IS NSSP GA KJE TS KSW GJWAP. ZRW CW ECET'W QJWWAP ZAUJRIA GA KJE TS ZJWKWRZ WS NRW CW CT JTMGJM.

—WSQ EPAAIAT

237

AUT YBTLYCT KTEFOI OM MTBTE OEFUTM IQEC, ROAU VSMA Y UYID-OEFU TLYMTL—OE FYMT ZQS AUQSCUA QKAOXOMX RYM JTYJ.

—LQHTLA HLYSIA

235 H represents A

236 P represents R

237 E represents N

235

Life is like a B-movie. You don't want to leave in the middle of it, but you don't want to see it again.

—Ted Turner

236

We were so poor we had no hot water. But it didn't matter because we had no bathtub to put it in anyway.

—Tom Dreesen

237

The average pencil is seven inches long, with just a half-inch eraser—in case you thought optimism was dead.

—Robert Brault

238

DRPP ZPRQOMQ'H KMYGRNQ BMPRZS GEBGYRGQZG HOGUH UXRQPS KYMU WXLRQN DYGXTKXHO XO OWG RQOGYQXORMQXP WMAHG MK BXQZXTGH.

—BXO DAZWXQXQ

239

STCHC KTWNEL MC KWYC KBTWWEK BJEECL LCVWHYJSWHACK SW XTABT UCWUEC JHC KCOS AV STCZ JHC SWW PWWL SW MC UHJBSABJE.

—KJYNCE MNSECH

240

JU AWZ SC YW YXFR YW UWK, XEB UWKG AWZ SC YW FSCYDE. SH UWK HSESCO HSGCY, VFDXCD FDY JD REWM.

—OXGGU ODGCOHSDFB

238 M represents O
239 E represents L
240 D represents E

238

Bill Clinton's foreign policy experience stems mainly from having breakfast at the International House of Pancakes.

—Pat Buchanan

239

There should be some schools called deformatories to which people are sent if they are too good to be practical.

—Samuel Butler

240

My job is to talk to you, and your job is to listen. If you finish first, please let me know.

—Harry Hershfield

241

SAQ SL BM ZYVQL TQRTQIX JDTVAR BM MQWTX VA IYQ IYQWIQT VX IYWI V ZSDOJA'I XVI VA IYQ WDJVQAZQ WAJ HWIZY BQ.

—KSYA EWTTMBSTQ

242

F ANVQ QH B YNOQBWYBVQ QGBQ ONYPNO LYNBJMBOQ BQ BVD QFSN. OH F HYTNYNT MYNVUG QHBOQ TWYFVX QGN YNVBFOOBVUN.

—OQNPNV AYFXGQ

243

VMND PNRR SFWFZ AF T QNWNRNIFY QHBSVZU BSVNR PF DOFSY JHZF JHSFU LHZ AHHXD VMTS PF YH LHZ QMFPNSE EBJ.

—FRAFZV MBAATZY

241 J represents D   242 F represents I   243 Q represents C

241

One of my chief regrets during my years in the theater is that I couldn't sit in the audience and watch me.

—John Barrymore

242

I went to a restaurant that serves breakfast at any time. So I ordered French toast during the Renaissance.

—Steven Wright

243

This will never be a civilized country until we spend more money for books than we do for chewing gum.

—Elbert Hubbard

244

ARYFCG AH ARI BFAIPGAYAI RBLRVYU GUGAIJ, BA BG FHV DHGGBZEI AH APYOIE XPHJ THYGA AH THYGA VBARHWA GIIBFL YFUARBFL.

—TRYPEIG CWPYEA

245

ZAZ ENJ VOVT GYQB AD Y TNNU YDZ CNTSVF GRE ENJ GYQBVZ AD? A FRADB FRYF'H RNG ZNSH HWVDZ FRVAT QAOVH.

—HJV UJTWRE

246

WUBYN YAB VWSB AYRRWGN. PTE IBG Y LTEOVB YCU VBYAC QTX GT QYCUVB GQBJ, YCU OABGGP NTTC PTE QYZB Y UTFBC.

—HTQC NGBWCRBLS

244 I represents E 245 Z represents D 246 A represents R

244

Thanks to the Interstate Highway System, it is now possible to travel from coast to coast without seeing anything.

—Charles Kuralt

245

Did you ever walk in a room and forget why you walked in? I think that's how dogs spend their lives.

—Sue Murphy

246

Ideas are like rabbits. You get a couple and learn how to handle them, and pretty soon you have a dozen.

—John Steinbeck

247

Z FCPHK'Y LHMGLYHI NA NZBBZKT WLHIZY WCLI YG YFH MGJZWH QHWCEBH SFGHPHL BYGJH ZY ZB BMHKIZKT JHBB YFCK NA SZDH.

—ZJZH KCBYCBH

248

OXK DKAO FZC OG BKKW HXLTSQKR XGVK LA OG VZBK OXK XGVK ZOVGAWXKQK WTKZAZRO—ZRS TKO OXK ZLQ GIO GY OXK OLQKA.

—SGQGOXC WZQBKQ

249

VMS JMTWAO UDTUAD ET TWZ FHO UFS ZT JDD NFO KTIBDJ VMDH ZMDS QFH JZFS FZ MTKD FHO JDD NFO ZDADIBJBTH GTP HTZMBHE?

—JFKWDA ETAOVSH

247 M represents P | 248 R represents N | 249 M represents H

247

I haven't reported my missing credit card to the police because whoever stole it is spending less than my wife.

—Ilie Nastase

248

The best way to keep children home is to make the home atmosphere pleasant—and let the air out of the tires.

—Dorothy Parker

249

Why should people go out and pay to see bad movies when they can stay at home and see bad television for nothing?

—Samuel Goldwyn

250

TMGELP T FXYGELP FYEVCY FOTV OC VOELGM TAXNV HYEVEHM EM ZEGC TMGELP T ZTIBBXMV OXF EV DCCZM TAXNV QXPM.

—HOYEMVXBOCY OTIBVXL

251

S'Z ESYX PT VXX PNX CTAXGKJXKP CXP TWP TU OMG MEPTCXPNXG MKZ EXMAX PNX ONTEX USXEZ PT HGSAMPX SKZWVPGQ.

—RTVXHN NXEEXG

252

RSPQXW, FE GFTKPX, JDP LJX YXPL GDPLSQA. SE JX RFXPQ'L OSVX DQ DGLFK JX PSIHOW LXDKP JSI TH.

—DOEKXR JSLGJGFGV

250 F represents W

251 E represents L

252 F represents O

250

Asking a working writer what he thinks about critics is like asking a lamppost how it feels about dogs.

—Christopher Hampton

251

I'd like to see the government get out of war altogether and leave the whole field to private industry.

—Joseph Heller

252

Disney, of course, has the best casting. If he doesn't like an actor he simply tears him up.

—Alfred Hitchcock

253

F CVTOY OCPL VODCWSZ CXSEW LFV HZOQOZODPOV QSZ WLO HZOVFYODPM, CDY DFDOWM-VFA VODCWSZV OCPL ZOPOFROY SDO RSWO.

—BSLD Q. TODDOYM

254

KZBBTR MPR: USRI LQO'GR SQKR QI NMAOGBML IZPSA, ASR ARTRDSQIR GZIPN, MIB LQO SQDR ZA'N ASR UGQIP IOKJRG.

—GZIP TMGBIRG

255

L CILGD YZG BIR IWFZ W MLZTNZJ ZWT WTZ VZCCZT MTZMWTZJ KRT YWTTLWEZ. CIZU'FZ ZPMZTLZGNZJ MWLG WGJ VRHEIC OZBZQTU.

—TLCW THJGZT

253

I asked each senator about his preferences for the presidency, and ninety-six senators each received one vote.

—John F. Kennedy

254

Middle age: when you're home on Saturday night, the telephone rings, and you hope it's the wrong number.

—Ring Lardner

255

I think men who have a pierced ear are better prepared for marriage. They've experienced pain and bought jewelry.

—Rita Rudner

256

VEI'LR ETNV QRLR JEL U WQELC KDWDC. SET'C QILLV. SET'C HELLV. UTS ZR WILR CE WGRNN CQR JNEHRLW UNETF CQR HUV.

—HUNCRL QUFRT

257

QEYYEBOU YBOZ LBK EQQBKXFYEXR SVB MB OBX HOBS SVFX XB MB SEXV XVJQUJYNJU BO F KFEOR UDOMFR FLXJKOBBO.

—UDUFO JKXW

258

ND PRJ RCQ PRJL KHUT H VJUSLQS IRJUSE, PRJ VHBQ H ILRKFQX; KJZ ND PRJ RCQ PRJL KHUT H XNFFNRU, NZ VHE.

—ARVU XHPUHLS TQPUQE

256 V represents Y

257 F represents A

258 N represents I

256

You're only here for a short visit. Don't hurry. Don't worry. And be sure to smell the flowers along the way.

—Walter Hagen

257

Millions long for immortality who do not know what to do with themselves on a rainy Sunday afternoon.

—Susan Ertz

258

If you owe your bank a hundred pounds, you have a problem; but if you owe your bank a million, it has.

—John Maynard Keynes

259

QTJ UNXQJXQ SNC QK XZGGJJL AX QK MKKY NX AU CKZ NFJ HMNCAWP VC KQTJF HJKHMJ'X FZMJX, STAMJ EZAJQMC HMNCAWP VC CKZF KSW.

—OAGTNJM YKFLN

260

EFDC FU OBFOEB DIZKG DIBN'MB LIYMZDYJEB ZU DIBN PZHB YSYN DIBZM FEX LEFDIBC YKX DIZKPC DIBN XFK'D SYKD.

—VNMDEB MBBX

261

ANZXZ'H HM YQVN KJIHAFV FE ANFH VQJAQXZ ANIA BFESJ JZMKIXP HUFE FH GZVMYFER IE ZEPIERZXZP HSEANZAFV.

—JFJS AMYJFE

259 Z represents U

260 Y represents A

261 V represents C

259

The fastest way to succeed is to look as if you are playing by other people's rules, while quietly playing by your own.

—Michael Korda

260

Lots of people think they're charitable if they give away their old clothes and things they don't want.

—Myrtle Reed

261

There's so much plastic in this culture that vinyl leopard skin is becoming an endangered synthetic.

—Lily Tomlin

262

LE CDZ QLMX YD YWX ITX DE I WZOSFXS CDZ WIMX LY GISX VXNIZAX MXFC EXP KXDKQX SLX KIAY YWX ITX DE I WZOSFXS.

—TXDFTX VZFOA

263

ZIKGUVHV VGACN IXSTH CUCAHQ GAKLACH SJ HZAUK OUMAV HTCUCW HZAUK ZIKGV ICN HAC GAKLACH GOIQUCW STH SJ HTCA.

—UWSK VHKIMUCVYQ

264

UYAIKLP ZG CUFUYC L TZVUIURULY INK HKDA IZ INK RUID, UI QUCNI EK EKIIKX IZ RNLYCK INK VZRHA.

—PZSC VLXAZY

262 M represents V | 263 I represents A | 264 R represents C

262

If you live to the age of a hundred you have it made because very few people die past the age of a hundred.

—George Burns

263

Harpists spend about ninety percent of their lives tuning their harps and ten percent playing out of tune.

—Igor Stravinsky

264

Instead of giving a politician the keys to the city, it might be better to change the locks.

—Doug Larson

265

NZCCOYZZA'U M FCMJH YNHVH BNHO'CC FMO OZT M BNZTUMLA AZCCMVU QZV M PWUU, MLA QWQBO JHLBU QZV OZTV UZTC.

—EMVWCOL EZLVZH

266

AN VSM XMHMJ GKFPNX, AJTE GAIME SFG F XSFHMJ NFOM. VSDX XSACTG VMTT CX XABMVSDJQ FRACV VSM OCXVAB AN XSFHDJQ.

—VAB PARRDJX

267

I HAVE LEFT ORDERS TO BE AWAKENED AT
U CEHN YNAK PBXNBF KP TN EVEQNRNX EK
ANY TIME IN CASE OF NATIONAL EMERGENCY
ERD KUIN UR SEFN PA REKUPREY NINBMNRSD,
EVEN IF I M IN A CABINET MEETING
NHNR UA U'I UR E SETURNK INNKURM.

RONALD REAGAN
—BPREYX BNEMER

265 T represents U **266** J represents N **267** S represents C

265

Hollywood's a place where they'll pay you a thousand dollars for a kiss, and fifty cents for your soul.

—Marilyn Monroe

266

Of the seven dwarfs, only Dopey had a shaven face. This should tell us something about the custom of shaving.

—Tom Robbins

267

I have left orders to be awakened at any time in case of national emergency, even if I'm in a cabinet meeting.

—Ronald Reagan

268

C KROCJIQR YJFD BCX PD RQD KQMORDKR TJKRCFED PDRVDDF RVM SMJFRK, PZR JR JK PX FM BDCFK RQD BMKR JFRDODKRJFI.

—TMERMO VQM

269

X'Y TKLKZVXW KOVGE NHNLPEJXZS. VZ YP MEKEXVZKLP OXIPIQN X JKHN K LNKLHXNC YXLLVL.

—LXIJKLW QNCXM

270

J TIIF DZWKVXVS ZW XIK WIGVIXV NZKP XIKPZXT KI WJU. J TIIF DZWKVXVS ZW J TIIF KJDQVS NZKP J WISV KPSIJK.

—QJKPJSZXV NPZKVPISX

268 B represents M | 269 P represents Y | 270 S represents R

268

A straight line may be the shortest distance between two points, but it is by no means the most interesting.

—Doctor Who

269

I'm paranoid about everything. On my stationary bicycle I have a rearview mirror.

—Richard Lewis

270

A good listener is not someone with nothing to say. A good listener is a good talker with a sore throat.

—Katharine Whitehorn

271

ZUYUDAUYO DSWPYV UY FAS PQJXNUWD OSFD JPL DUQISK. ZUYUDAUYO DSWPYV UY NPQUFUWD OSFD JPL PTQUIUPY.

—KUWACKV XUQAPLD YUBPY

272

E FA PWX MEKKEPT XW SECN XOZ KEYZC WR TZSAFP CWKHEZSC RWS BWQPXSEZC MOWCZ PFAZC MZ BFPPWX CDZKK DSWDZSKL.

—YWKNZS SQOZ

273

PRF KGZQFTP BGUJ YZ PRF FZQKYTR KDZQMDQF YT PRF GZF PRDP WGKKGBT PRF NRUDTF, "DZJ ZGB D BGUJ WUGL GMU TNGZTGU."

—RDK FDPGZ

271 S represents E

272 W represents O

273 B represents W

271

Finishing second in the Olympics gets you silver. Finishing second in politics gets you oblivion.

—Richard Milhous Nixon

272

I am not willing to risk the lives of German soldiers for countries whose names we cannot spell properly.

—Volker Ruhe

273

The longest word in the English language is the one that follows the phrase, "And now a word from our sponsor."

—Hal Eaton

274

LKLG WUAL LFVYOLAVZMGE ZPVG ZPL EQI BPU ZPMGSY PL SGUBY MZ VRR MY ZPL UGL BPU ALVRRI NULY.

—VR CLAGYZLMG

275

J EDMP HEFRXB LQ ZJGC I CPB EY HIBBPUJPC YEU MXUJCBLIC VJBX I DEBP ED JB CIQJDR, “BEQC DEB JDMTFGPG.”

—HPUDIUG LIDDJDR

276

PWLCFUOH DUO GWO IVTG FOTLUDXCO VNNVHOHGT DG TPUDXXCO DT GWOA DUO XVGW ODTA GV XODG DHF RZH GV PWODG.

—RUDH COXVSLGE

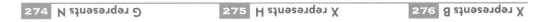

274 G represents N   275 X represents H   276 X represents B

274

Even more exasperating than the guy who thinks he knows it all is the one who really does.

—Al Bernstein

275

I once bought my kids a set of batteries for Christmas with a note on it saying, "Toys not included."

—Bernard Manning

276

Children are the most desirable opponents at Scrabble as they are both easy to beat and fun to cheat.

—Fran Lebowitz

277

IZX VAWN SLBV IAX HZUKO BPZ XAWHK'O JWZUBZOB SLBLZO LI BPZ IDQEZW AT MZAMHZ UWADIK XPAQ VAD OPADHKI'B QUNZ U ODKKZI QARZ.

—KURLK HZBBZWQUI

278

DAG TU QBKTL LBMW BM HAN JUKMBMW? BH'L HAN HKBXJSAIMH LAUXH: "DN WUH HAKUXWA IMUHANK MBWAH."

—NMBT QIWMUOT

279

UN UOV VRRZDZPQQS WPQMN RKNNHVL VR AINNDO PFVWN QZRN ZEANQR ANNL EV OPWN YVEOZYJ EV EPQC PFVME FME EON UNPEONK.

—FPKFPKP NOKNYKNZDO

277 Q represents M

278 W represents G

279 R represents F

277

New York City now leads the world's greatest cities in the number of people around whom you shouldn't make a sudden move.

—David Letterman

278

Why do birds sing in the morning? It's the triumphant shout: "We got through another night."

—Enid Bagnold

279

We who officially value freedom of speech above life itself seem to have nothing to talk about but the weather.

—Barbara Ehrenreich

280

XKA X QXF PGBSG PXJ GL BK VDBFV ZD RDZL, XFI GL PBWW TNDCXCWJ ZLWW JDE. XKA GBQ, GDPLRLN, PGJ, XFI RXVELFLKK BK XWW.

—CLNFXNI WLRBF

281

DUKPLVLA GQXW EQXCK MEVUK GQXW SVBC PWK CZVUU AWQMVLA VC UVSK CEQRKUVLA ZEK MPUS JKNQWK VZ CZQIC CLQMVLA.

—IEGUUVC BVUUKW

282

E THRXPHRDVY DV QGY EPQ HU CDKDCDZW E TEFY DZ VITG E AEN QGEQ YKYPNHZY MYBDYKYV GY GEV QGY MDWWYVQ XDYTY.

—BICADW YPGEPC

280 R represents V

281 U represents L

282 T represents C

280

Ask a man which way he is going to vote, and he will probably tell you. Ask him, however, why, and vagueness is all.

—Bernard Levin

281

Cleaning your house while your kids are still growing is like shoveling the walk before it stops snowing.

—Phyllis Diller

282

A compromise is the art of dividing a cake in such a way that everyone believes he has the biggest piece.

—Ludwig Erhard

283

O'K S DVOZBNBDVG KSTBQ. PVSP KYSIN O FSI PVOIE WYYD PVBJXVPN SMBJP MYOIX JIYKDZBGYW.

—MQJFY ZYY

284

VD INWWTCNNJ, ED GUFVLEXWG JVONHKG MGLLWGAGDL AGEDM GEKI REHLT BGLLVDB PVPLT RGHKGDL NP LIG RFXWVKVLT.

—WEFHGD XEKEWW

285

PMQJ ECQD MWJ M RQCROQ LQMKO CL KAWJ RQORMQO ZCN LCQ VPO GNFDZ UQOMDH VPMV LAWMGGZ FCKO MGCWT—CQ JCW'V.

—PMQQAHCW LCQJ

283 D represents P 284 V represents I 285 K represents M

283

I'm a philosophy major. That means I can think deep thoughts about being unemployed.

—Bruce Lee

284

In Hollywood, an equitable divorce settlement means each party getting fifty percent of the publicity.

—Lauren Bacall

285

Hard work and a proper frame of mind prepare you for the lucky breaks that finally come along—or don't.

—Harrison Ford

286

W'FJ QVWUJM V RJE ZNTUMC VGNTUM HAJ PWMMKJ. HAJ NUKB KNEJG-ONMB QVGPJUHC W NEU HAVH CHWKK RWH PJ YNPRNGHVOKB VGJ HNEJKC.

—MVFJ OVGGB

287

SHIHK AKMP MAJTX ZJTK MSLHYXJKY LJEQSP JIHK JS XCH EMZODJVHK; XCH QEEQPKMXQJS DMVY VHKHS'X MY YXKQLX QS XCJYH NMZY.

—DHV DHCK

288

ZF'C CFAIQBN WKY LNY KL FWN YKAUT'C BANIF MAKRUNHC IAN CKUJNT RG MNKMUN YWK ANHNHRNA FWNZA IUBNRAI.

—WNARNAF MAKDWQKY

286 E represents W

287 X represents T

288 R represents B

286

I've gained a few pounds around the middle. The only lower-body garments I own that still fit me comfortably are towels.

—Dave Barry

287

Never brag about your ancestors coming over on the Mayflower; the immigration laws weren't as strict in those days.

—Lew Lehr

288

It's strange how few of the world's great problems are solved by people who remember their algebra.

—Herbert Prochnow

289

IVXC FKPC QKZCA UXJCIFN, EJIOKXI RBWWCVA KV TFBAOJWD FJDOIA. JT NKX OCBV RCFFA, DCI NKXV CBVA QOCQMCY.

—CVJQO ACDBF

290

IF YOU DONT WANT TO WORK YOU HAVE TO
SR DHM CHU'J XBUJ JH XHNA, DHM GBKV JH
WORK TO EARN ENOUGH MONEY SO THAT YOU
XHNA JH VBNU VUHMFG EHUVD OH JGBJ DHM
WONT HAVE TO WORK
XHU'J GBKV JH XHNA.

OGDEN NASH
—HFCVU UBOG

291

NWZONAZUNJA NM Z OJJV LJPMG UJ KZPPH HJR JSGP ULG OPJRAV—AJU Z DCHNAO KZPXGU UJ MGU HJR DPGG DPJW XPJTZTNCNUH.

—PJTGPUMJA VZSNGM

289 X represents U — 290 X represents W — 291 O represents G

289

True love comes quietly, without banners or flashing lights. If you hear bells, get your ears checked.

—Erich Segal

290

If you don't want to work, you have to work to earn enough money so that you won't have to work.

—Ogden Nash

291

Imagination is a good horse to carry you over the ground—not a flying carpet to set you free from probability.

—Robertson Davies

292

JEQBDP JFO JBTJWP JPZGHX BGDDBO ZGEP TKJD DKOW TJHD DL NO TKOH DKOW XFLT QV—'AJQPO DKOW'FO BLLZGHX MLF GEOJP.

—VJQBJ VLQHEPDLHO

293

L ZETUQCZ QC L XBRREY YNE IUQABC ZNETCLPIC EX FQRBC CE NB JLP WB GNEZEOULGNBI CZLPIQPO QP XUEPZ EX NQC JLU.

—BFQRB OLPBCZ

294

REI'J RJ EJGKIVC? JFC EKTC OCXOHC MFX HKAVF KJ VWOEW BXGJAIC JCHHCGE JKDC CQXIXTREJE ECGRXAEHW.

—QRIQRIIKJR CIYARGCG

292 Z represents K | 293 Z represents T | 294 V represents G

292

Adults are always asking little kids what they want to be when they grow up—'cause they're looking for ideas.

—Paula Poundstone

293

A tourist is a fellow who drives thousands of miles so he can be photographed standing in front of his car.

—Emile Ganest

294

Isn't it strange? The same people who laugh at gypsy fortune tellers take economists seriously.

—Cincinnati Enquirer

295

HSZXSB ANX KHZK IJKGSBKKUBS YBHC GS THLOK, SXO TGLOGXS, NHK SBMBQ QBHY XCY TGMB-ZBHQ VQXDBLOGXSK.

—UHCLXCU TXQIBK

296

Q'K FQSJP VM WGG FLQY DVDYJDYJ WNVTF NJWTFI NJQDZ VDGI YEQD PJJH. FLWF'Y PJJH JDVTZL. XLWF PV IVT XWDF, WD WPVSWNGJ HWDRSJWY?

—BJWD EJSS

297

SXNJHPG JWLOSWN RN JSLJ DWU LUY ULJXHUN TWSLCW FXNWBG HUOW JSWG SLCW WQSLRNJWY LBB HJSWP LBJWPULJXCWN.

—LTTL WTLU

295 T represents F **296** N represents B **297** G represents Y

295

Anyone who says businessmen deal in facts, not fiction, has never read old five-year projections.

—Malcolm Forbes

296

I'm tired of all this nonsense about beauty being only skin deep. That's deep enough. What do you want, an adorable pancreas?

—Jean Kerr

297

History teaches us that men and nations behave wisely once they have exhausted all other alternatives.

—Abba Eban

298

VGZD ELZ IPXQU EFED FXVG ILXMZ-XQB. QPF FGZLZ ELZ VGZ VZZQEUZLB UPXQU VP UP VP QPV FEVNG E RPMXZ?

—TPT VGPREB

299

GZIV GZH FHYNGZ SZ O RUGLNOZP SN O QGYH, OZP UH SN SZRHYHNRSZJ QHMOLNH UH SN GZH FHYNGZ SZ O RUGLNOZP.

—UOYGIP ZSMGINGZ

300

KRSP HP HDI SCPM CV VGMYW WIOCYX WH PCYF VHLMWKCYX WH FH UCWK WKM WCLM UM KRQM IDVKMF WKIHDXK SCPM WIOCYX WH VRQM.

—UCSS IHXMIV

298 F represents W 299 G represents O 300 X represents G

298

They are doing away with drive-ins. Now where are the teenagers going to go to not watch a movie?

—Bob Thomas

299

Only one person in a thousand is a bore, and he is interesting because he is one person in a thousand.

—Harold Nicolson

300

Half of our life is spent trying to find something to do with the time we have rushed through life trying to save.

—Will Rogers

301

XZY CFKCHXCSY EO ZCKQHS C ACF VYVEIU QN XZCX, NYKYICW XQVYN EKYI, EHY YHGEUN XZY NCVY SEEF XZQHSN OEI XZY OQINX XQVY.

—OIQYFIQJZ HQYXDNJZY

302

JMUX, AJ KJB LUBH LUI VQEAS, WYS BJHAI'S HRHEXJIH LUMH U EJYKG BEUVS WHVJEH SGHX LUMH U LUASHENQHFH?

—FJYESIHX GYASJI

303

QP KEKAKNO DXTGBETX INT AB TSX WXD ZBD HXZNQNAKBE BZ UWNDNUAXD, YSA AWXE K DXNOKRXH AWNA K WNH EB UWNDNUAXD.

—UWNDOXT YNDVOXP

301 K represents V **302** L represents M **303** B represents O

301

The advantage of having a bad memory is that, several times over, one enjoys the same good things for the first time.

—Friedrich Nietzsche

302

Okay, so God made man first, but doesn't everyone make a rough draft before they make a masterpiece?

—Courtney Huston

303

My initial response was to sue her for defamation of character, but then I realized that I had no character.

—Charles Barkley

304

CVXGVYW DOVTVT VT MBUM CZCWIM PBWI QZS OWUGVFW QZSO DBVGXOWI UIX QZSO DGZMBWT UOW UKZSM MBW TUCW UNW.

—KVGG MUCCWST

305

YHRTMBUQD PWNN KUCUQ QUTNJYU BEU PJDBULJDOUB PEUK WB YHRUD BH DBQUJRNWKWKZ HSSWYU PHQO.

—YNJVBHK UNPUNN

306

ECYOY SD HKECSHA XKOY XSDYOBZRY SH ECYFKORP ECBH EK BOOSNY SH WBOBPSDY BHP RKKQ RSQY UKVO WBDDWKOE WCKEK.

—YOXB ZKXZYGQ

304 G represents L   305 Y represents C   306 W represents P

304

Midlife crisis is that moment when you realize your children and your clothes are about the same age.

—Bill Tammeus

305

Computers will never replace the wastebasket when it comes to streamlining office work.

—Clayton Elwell

306

There is nothing more miserable in the world than to arrive in paradise and look like your passport photo.

—Erma Bombeck

307

VMJ VKTOAZJ ISVM WTYV TP OY SY VMNV IJ ITOZR KNVMJK AJ KOSFJR AL DKNSYJ VMNF YNQJR AL UKSVSUSYW.

—FTKWNF QSFUJFV DJNZJ

308

UPTMEVS LGUZ OP MEV EXQUP DEUSUDMVS OH MEUM VIVSKWTFK ZUPMH MT WXOGF UPF PTWTFK ZUPMH MT FT QUOPMVPUPDV.

—JXSM ITPPVAXM

309

MEB JBLXBNNPTC MEPTC WYSRM MBTTPN PN MEWM TS AWMMBX ESF CSSJ P CBM, P'DD TBZBX YB WN CSSJ WN W FWDD.

—APMUE EBJYBXC

307 K represents R

308 V represents E

309 C represents G

307

The trouble with most of us is that we would rather be ruined by praise than saved by criticism.

—Norman Vincent Peale

308

Another flaw in the human character is that everybody wants to build and nobody wants to do maintenance.

—Kurt Vonnegut

309

The depressing thing about tennis is that no matter how good I get, I'll never be as good as a wall.

—Mitch Hedberg

310

YA TDV JZB KABXKJ BNA DPPAFBHZJ ZP BNZLA YNZ CHEA XL, OXB YA DCYDVL KALUAFB BNAHK QZZI WXIQTAJB.

—CHOOHA PXIHT

311

CSDB ASMZQV HZC DJHLPICLME VICDA ME RQMCSDA AM TD TMZQV YEMT TSDE CSDB KM MZC MN ACBQD.

—KIPPB ASIEVQLEK

312

P GSIY YD T BPRB XABDDC YBTY GTX XD MTIRSFDJX, YBS XABDDC ISGXWTWSF BTM TI DOPYJTFQ ADCJVI.

—FDANQ FTQ

310 K represents R

311 S represents H

312 P represents I

310

We may not return the affection of those who like us, but we always respect their good judgment.

—Libbie Fudim

311

They should put expiration dates on clothes so we would know when they go out of style.

—Garry Shandling

312

I went to a high school that was so dangerous, the school newspaper had an obituary column.

—Rocky Ray

313

DPWH-FXDMXKWXEP XD BYPE VAGT MAEDMXPEMP QPWWD VAG QA FA DASPQYXEJ REF VAG FAE'Q QRWL ZRML.

—B.L. YAKP

314

KFECJ KX UMLC JEB GBJ Q XBKA UKAM AUE ZQKFX EV ZQCAX, QCI AMLC GBFC Q MEPL KC AML DEQA.

—PQBFLCDL ZLALF

315

V GWHAWU'N USEDAVALWJ LN FVGS RT AYS JDFRSU WQ SFLJSJA FSJ KYW GLS DJGSU YLN HVUS.

—CSWUCS RSUJVUG NYVK

313 D represents S

314 L represents E

315 A represents T

313

Self-discipline is when your conscience tells you to do something and you don't talk back.

—W.K. Hope

314

Irony is when you buy a suit with two pairs of pants, and then burn a hole in the coat.

—Laurence Peter

315

A doctor's reputation is made by the number of eminent men who die under his care.

—George Bernard Shaw

316

A PADVYF UZFT JL ZVKHQTE WBJFK ZBJF PYBJ UBYO, AP CZF OAEK QYF KCASS QSAMF, CZFT A'MF EBTF JL RBH.

—YBKFQTTF QYTBSE

317

TIY DGL JT ATTV TXJ MTO YIBFIYYOL—JDYN PYBFI RFJD LYRFIB CGQDFIYL GIK YIK XH RFJD JDY GJTCFQ PTCP.

—CGOQYA HGBITA

318

EB E MRRAEDRU, W ZEB LNUR NK EA EAEUQXWBM, OCM ANZ W ZEAM VRNVYR MN MXUWTR EAP OR XEULNAWNCB.

—AWQNYEB QEDR

316 J represents M **317** G represents A **318** X represents H

316

I figure when my husband comes home from work, if the kids are still alive, then I've done my job.

—Roseanne Arnold

317

One has to look out for engineers—they begin with sewing machines and end up with the atomic bomb.

—Marcel Pagnol

318

As a teenager, I was more of an anarchist, but now I want people to thrive and be harmonious.

—Nicolas Cage

319

LI WZNC, X EZYZC CZNVXUZW TING N GZCCXFVZ VLG LQ ZRSVNXEXEA LEZ INK GL WL XE N HMCWZC!

—NANGIN BICXKGXZ

320

T KILPAIO NR CMN NWI NRTKIN FILN ORYA. TN XLJIF SRM KRRJ KTJI L YLPX, BLPTAZ, FIAFTNTQI WMXLA GITAZ.

—PLKCW ARGKI

321

BMJBWH DP VQYP SC SLCHP WCIVFPX SLBV WCI, DPYBIHP SLPW BXP SLP CVPH JLC JQMM DP JXQSQVF BDCIS WCI.

—YWXQM YCVVCMMW

319 W represents D

320 X represents M

321 D represents B

319

Oh dear, I never realized what a terrible lot of explaining one has to do in a murder!

—Agatha Christie

320

I learned to put the toilet seat down. It makes you look like a warm, caring, sensitive human being.

—Ralph Noble

321

Always be nice to those younger than you, because they are the ones who will be writing about you.

—Cyril Connolly

322

W OWYMKH PWBWFMQG MR QGA JXACA HQZ WCCMPA JMFX OMPA EWVR, OQZC DMIR WGI RAPAG M-FXQZVXF-HQZ-TWBDAI-MFR.

—MPACG EWKK

323

HKO ISJCH CSLW GI NYHBJSHQ SC HKO TSCDGUOJQ HKYH HKO UGPBNO AWGE YPCG HBJWC HG HKO POIH.

—DKSDYLG HJSEBWO

324

MWS BNC'G NPUNME IW XM VTJVAG WJKCKWC. N GSAZVM, KH MWS NEZ N GSAZVM, ERWSPL XV EGSHHVL UKGR IANEERWJJVAE, IAKG NCL UWAOE.

—NCWCMOWSE

322 P represents V

323 P represents L

324 J represents P

322

A family vacation is one where you arrive with five bags, four kids and seven I-thought-you-packed-its.

—Ivern Ball

323

The first sign of maturity is the discovery that the volume knob also turns to the left.

—Chicago Tribune

324

You can't always go by expert opinion. A turkey, if you ask a turkey, should be stuffed with grasshoppers, grit and worms.

—Anonymous

325

LYCCKYJS KG QKXS DAKCQKPJ Y IYDVP, DZCPKPJ FYPOGMCKPJG, VC SYDKPJ AKDF BFVMGDKBXG. KD QVVXG SYGR ZPDKQ RVZ DCR KD.

—FSQSP CVAQYPO

326

TWKI XPN FKCJW GPF LWK ZLCFZ, XPN YCX IPL ONRLK QKL PIK, ANL XPN TPI'L JPYK NB TRLW C WCISGNM PG YNS KRLWKF.

—MKP ANFIKLL

327

D ZBCT MF D LDP ENB FUTPVF FB LXIN AMLT ADWSMPJ DZBXA NMLFTWG ANDA OBX IDP'A ADWS DZBXA OBXCFTWG.

—LTWQMWWT WDPVBP

325 X represents K

326 Y represents M

327 T represents E

325

Marriage is like twirling a baton, turning handsprings, or eating with chopsticks. It looks easy until you try it.

—Helen Rowland

326

When you reach for the stars, you may not quite get one, but you won't come up with a handful of mud either.

—Leo Burnett

327

A bore is a man who spends so much time talking about himself that you can't talk about yourself.

—Melville Landon

328

QAPP HWZ JZEJPZ AG HWZ BWZUJZT FZUHF BPUJ DERT WUGSF? UPP HWZ TZFH EO DER, AO DER'PP XRFH TUHHPZ DERT XZQZPTD.

—XEWG PZGGEG

329

P OLSTQLO P'X MUQPW MJ KUZXPWQ Z ESUR MJ VLZHUVEUZKU, MTO OLUW P OLSTQLO, DLJ VLSTYX P? LU WUNUK KUZXV ZWJ SC RPWU.

—VEPHU RTYYPQZW

330

WZS NTVSG L YGNM, WZS TSHH LJFNGWCUW WZS ONJJC QSONJSH. TSW WZS GSCVSG OCWOZ ZLH NMU QGSCWZ.

—STLICQSWZ OTCGPHNU IMCGW

328 X represents J

329 W represents N

330 L represents I

328

Will the people in the cheaper seats clap your hands? All the rest of you, if you'll just rattle your jewelry.

—John Lennon

329

I thought I'd begin by reading a poem by Shakespeare, but then I thought, why should I? He never reads any of mine.

—Spike Mulligan

330

The older I grow, the less important the comma becomes. Let the reader catch his own breath.

—Elizabeth Clarkson Zwart

331

PMLOKTLOP KNO ROPK ZGI KM BMDYTDBO PMLOMDO NO TP ZFMDW TP KM AOK NTL NGYO NTP ZGI.

—FOS M'SMDDOAA

332

CVNAVME VF XVRO B FYVUOP'F JOK, BAABNQOU OLOP FM FXVIQAXH YOPQBYF, KZA FAVXX BAABNQOU AM XVCO BA BXX CMZP NMPEOPF.

—LVPIVEVB JMMXC

333

P UCNIZ LC TIA ECBV WPLE RCB UE GIFHLG. P'U SFBFTCPZ FTZ TIA ECBV AFX LGI CTHE SHFWI AGIBI UE RIFBX AIBI QDXLPRPIZ.

—FTPLF AIPXX

331 G represents A
332 N represents C
333 F represents A

331

Sometimes the best way to convince someone he is wrong is to let him have his way.

—Red O'Donnell

332

Fiction is like a spider's web, attached ever so slightly perhaps, but still attached to life at all four corners.

—Virginia Woolf

333

I moved to New York City for my health. I'm paranoid and New York was the only place where my fears were justified.

—Anita Weiss

334

SUE VYIYH GYY P NPV DPRBZVM QUDV CAY GCHYYC DZCA P DUNPV DAU APG P RZCCRY WUCLYRRS PVQ P LPRQ GWUC.

—YRPSVY LUUGRYH

335

QS KRPOMLTB GVJRZ PN MR ATXIZ XVR QS IGEKQTERB GKZ P UTIZ MPQ TN ATXBVR MR ATXIZ, VT ITKO GV MR ZPZK'U UGJR PU TXU TN QS OGBZRK.

—RBPA QTBRAGQLR

336

ULM MB UZH ZYAXHJU LMAXJ SF UZH HFRKSJZ KYFRGYRH UM AZCNH YAH KSBH YFX KMWH—MB YKK LMAXJ.

—JUHDZHF JMFXZHSN

334 D represents W 335 O represents G 336 X represents D

334

You never see a man walking down the street with a woman who has a little potbelly and a bald spot.

—Elayne Boosler

335

My neighbor asked if he could use my lawnmower and I told him of course he could, so long as he didn't take it out of my garden.

—Eric Morecambe

336

Two of the hardest words in the English language to rhyme are life and love—of all words.

—Stephen Sondheim

337

SRCMCZCA L RCDA DMGBMC DAWHLMW OBA IEDZCAG, L OCCE D IJABMW LUNHEIC JB ICC LJ JALCF BM RLU NCAIBMDEEG.

—DKADRDU ELMVBEM

338

MTK WKNA FNGQKW VH GPM MTNM IPDRSMKWH ZVAA UKQVG MP MTVGX AVXK DKG, USM MTNM DKG ZVAA UKQVG MP MTVGX AVXK IPDRSMKWH.

—HEFGKE TNWWVH

339

HMEJ NF NXJMCY ZCAVCPCS EZXDJ QXXBVKO VI JMEJ VL FXD HXYBCS MEYS EKS GYXIGCYCS, IXNCXKC CAIC HXDAS SX VJ LXY FXD.

—KXYE CGMYXK

337 E represents L

338 D represents M

339 C represents E

337

Whenever I hear anyone arguing for slavery, I feel a strong impulse to see it tried on him personally.

—Abraham Lincoln

338

The real danger is not that computers will begin to think like men, but that men will begin to think like computers.

—Sydney Harris

339

What my mother believed about cooking is that if you worked hard and prospered, someone else would do it for you.

—Nora Ephron

340

BRT UYTV MYO UTITMU QIYM XTBSV, NQO QIYM OTCITSBCTMO BMU WTBAOW. VYCT CTM BST NYSM YAU, BMU VYCT MTHTS RSYP VY.

—OSXYM TUPBSUV

341

R KCWPCT WRE USTL OJF VJFPRYMF, USP RE RTWOJPMWP WRE CEBL RKQJFM OJF WBJMEP PC ZBREP QJEMF.

—HTREY BBCLK NTJIOP

342

CM NPF JGCDJ PSS NOGDJ PM RH ZGSSVJV CDMVOTCVN IDMCS C DGDZLPSPDMSH PFYVE, “EG HGI DVVE PDH SPOJV EGDPMCGDF AGO DVN KICSECDJF?”

—MGEE PDEVOFGD

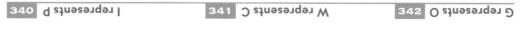

340 I represents P 341 W represents C 342 G represents O

340

Age does not depend upon years, but upon temperament and health. Some men are born old, and some never grow so.

—Tryon Edwards

341

A doctor can bury his mistakes, but an architect can only advise his client to plant vines.

—Frank Lloyd Wright

342

It was going all wrong at my college interview until I nonchalantly asked, “Do you need any large donations for new buildings?”

—Todd Anderson

343

QE QF FRXVGA ECNE GOR MNUEF GO TGGV ERUAF, IRLNKFR QZ GOR PRUR GO TGGV ERUAF GOR PGKXV OGE MNUE.

—ANULRX MUGKFE

344

HK UMLPMJ DEYW HW ROB HMCPGR PM AOYW, QVP XGWC O LMVAUC'P NEK PGW QOAA GW DEYW HW ROB HMCPGR HMJW.

—XEAPWJ HEPPGEV

345

PZFYF'N IXF PZBXM OTIDP QZBVSYFX—PZFE XFAFY MI OYIDXS NZIJBXM NXOHNZIPN IW PZFBY MYOXSHOYFXPN.

—TFNNBF & TFDVOZ

343 V represents D | 344 H represents M | 345 Y represents R

343

It is seldom that one parts on good terms, because if one were on good terms one would not part.

—Marcel Proust

344

My doctor gave me six months to live, but when I couldn't pay the bill he gave me six months more.

—Walter Matthau

345

There's one thing about children—they never go around showing snapshots of their grandparents.

—Bessie & Beulah

346

WHSW RO WZA LHLA HXRCRWM WP EAAD
ORCAVW UZRCA WUP YLRAVKO HLA HLIGRVI,
HVK MPG EVPU XPWZ PY WZAB HLA ULPVI.

—ZGIZ HCCAV

347

UGVMCMTC MT D RNSSQKAX KQDCS UK CMWB
VNDV SWDLXST D VSDHSVVXS VU TMWY
VNUAYN MW NUV JDVSQ AG VU MVT WUTS.

—NDQUXB NSXKSQ

348

FDFM KDFBVFQYXI URIA QMAIQMUIQDFCO
TMKV IXF URBNQMRC BHCF: VXFM LRI,
RBBRMYF OKHBAFCL QM ACQG ZKAFA.

—EKXM VFQIJ

346 U represents W

347 T represents S

348 K represents O

346

Tact is the rare ability to keep silent while two friends are arguing, and you know both of them are wrong.

—Hugh Allen

347

Optimism is a cheerful frame of mind that enables a teakettle to sing though in hot water up to its nose.

—Harold Helfer

348

Even overweight cats instinctively know the cardinal rule: when fat, arrange yourself in slim poses.

—John Weitz

349

LUWWUP OZPOZ MO VYZ WUOV ZBZPHN IMOVJMAXVZI TXGPVMVN MP VYZ EUJHI. ZBZJNUPZ VYMPQO YZ YGO ZPUXCY.

—JZPZ IZOLGJVZO

350

QTC RSXWQ QSNC S UCVQ QM BV BNCXSABV XCWQBGXBVQ, QTCF BWZCY, "TMU NBVF BXC SV FMGX DBXQF?" S WBSY, "QUM NSHHSMV."

—FBZMP WNSXVMRR

351

X ATFH SEPXKHL PATP PAH NHENGH ZAE TUH GTPH TUH EMPHS YE WJKA QEGGXHU PATS PAH NHENGH ZAE ATFH PE ZTXP MEU PAHW.

—H.F. GJKTY

349 N represents Y 350 F represents Y 351 S represents N

349

Common sense is the most evenly distributed quantity in the world. Everyone thinks he has enough.

—René Descartes

350

The first time I went to an American restaurant, they asked, "How many are in your party?" I said, "Two million."

—Yakov Smirnoff

351

I have noticed that the people who are late are often so much jollier than the people who have to wait for them.

—E.V. Lucas

352

LIRJNAEANU AD JGGYOAZF YZRDRGK NY XJSR XADNJSRD. JIN AD SZYOAZF OCALC YZRD NY SRRW.

—DLYNN JQJXD

353

MUTLJUO WIEJ I UIUJ QFMJU PFL STEJP LF IPGFPJ JKOJ; MJ VIP HFUJ QJFQKJ KFPS IDLJU MJ IUJ BJIB.

—OTPVKITU KJMTO

354

TNVIL N'GL KLIRSL X ILVBEXQ KXVJLE, N'GL QLXEVLW BR SASKQL HNBO ZELXB IROLELVIL.

—XQXV ZELLVTYXV

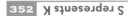

352 S represents K   353 K represents L   354 N represents I

352

Creativity is allowing oneself to make mistakes. Art is knowing which ones to keep.

—Scott Adams

353

Writers have a rare power not given to anyone else; we can bore people long after we are dead.

—Sinclair Lewis

354

Since I've become a central banker, I've learned to mumble with great coherence.

—Alan Greenspan

355

HFZHVF PRZ ROAF UZ PFONUFQQFQ OKF MFKKCEVF; MRFKF CQ UZ POD ZG MONCUS OIAOUMOSF ZG MRFW.

—OUOMZVF GKOUXF

356

VWN LNSCPR JPCV ENPEHN EHSX IPHO MC VP TNSL ZHPVWNC VWNX TPFHU RPV DN ZSFIWV UNSU MR PVWNLTMCN.

—LPINL CMJPR

357

OIBX BX V QCSS ZEMWOCG. QEPJX IVTS V CBKIO OE XSWF YS PSOOSCX, VWF B IVTS V CBKIO WEO OE CSVF OISY.

—HBPPBVY QVMPJWSC

355 P represents W

356 L represents R

357 W represents N

355

People who have no weaknesses are terrible; there is no way of taking advantage of them.

—Anatole France

356

The reason most people play golf is to wear clothes they would not be caught dead in otherwise.

—Roger Simon

357

This is a free country. Folks have a right to send me letters, and I have a right not to read them.

—William Faulkner

358

CSP RPZ CJ PKPEZCSAGH AV LNCAPGDP. ZJI HPC CSP DSADRPG QZ SNCDSAGH CSP PHH, GJC QZ VYNVSAGH AC.

—NEGJXM S. HXNVJO

359

NEQZA DBQY GCJ ZSQ ZYLSG ZYH GCJ DTKK UZAQ MBQ VQNM NEQQFB GCJ DTKK QIQS SQLSQM.

—ZUVSCNQ VTQSFQ

360

WSNU GEQ XEBU RP GUERSRA. PJ UBUR DPJMU, SI GEQ XEBU E GUERSRA PN DXSHX S VSMEKKJPBU.

—EMXWUSAX FJSWWSERI

358 D represents C 359 B represents H 360 B represents V

358

The key to everything is patience. You get the chicken by hatching the egg, not by smashing it.

—Arnold H. Glasow

359

Speak when you are angry and you will make the best speech you will ever regret.

—Ambrose Bierce

360

Life may have no meaning. Or even worse, it may have a meaning of which I disapprove.

—Ashleigh Brilliant

361

GQOT BOHBWO PJE LO DA D QPYO PTX JBPSO FQPTRO, D KOWW KQOL D QPYO DK PK QHLO DT LX JBPSO GPWWOK.

—TDFE PSTOKKO

362

D'AA ODFC KPV GJ DSCG PX ETGM ZDJS PX OVK TC EGR. RGDJM XUGJYDR EPVAS TGFC QVJYTCS TDN DJ MTC NPVMT.

—OCJC QCUUCM

363

DH ZED PTFF ZEVO E SXOEQ FOEROX PMH PEDQB QH RH TQ EFF MTZBOFC HX SOQ EFF QMO UXORTQ CHX RHTDS TQ.

—EDRXOP UEXDOSTO

361 T represents N

362 V represents U

363 R represents D

361

When people ask me if I have any spare change, I tell them I have it at home in my spare wallet.

—Nick Arnette

362

I'll give you an idea of what kind of guy he was. Saint Francis would have punched him in the mouth.

—Gene Perret

363

No man will make a great leader who wants to do it all himself or get all the credit for doing it.

—Andrew Carnegie

364

JYN DFFQM G'LF HFFB ZFAAGBT VGX BYZ ZY HWI SBIZVGBT JYN XI HGNZVKSI, SBK VF MZGAA JYNTYZ ZY HNGBT XF MYXFZVGBT.

—ZSBIS BYF

365

VYR E ZEJRVA SEPTR GKSC RHRUISCKQD XTNYR ES CEQL EQL LNQ'S UVYC; NSCRUGKYR INV'TT TNNJ TKJR E AESXCGNUJ FVKTS.

—TVXKTTR PETT

366

YGQ KGPL QLBKGO, B VGH GY MGVVAUGGW ZCT KMGHK BQL FIQCGIK HG KLL MGU HMLA'W ZL WQBUO UCHM ZIVTCOT LALK BOW OG FMCO.

—PBHH TQGLOCOT

364 H represents B　365 J represents K　366 U represents W

364

For weeks I've been telling him not to buy anything for my birthday, and he still forgot to bring me something.

—Tanya Noe

365

Use a makeup table with everything close at hand and don't rush; otherwise you'll look like a patchwork quilt.

—Lucille Ball

366

For some reason, a lot of Hollywood big shots are curious to see how they'd be drawn with bulging eyes and no chin.

—Matt Groening

367

RZVKV BKV FY DFFYWVFR XQARBFPVKA. NZBR NVKV RZVQ PYDFE RZVKV DF RZV UDKAR CGBWV?

—NDGGDBO A. XTKKYTEZA

368

N DNHK SKIUI DEH E WMPQ PM SKI SB SP STUM TX SKI NMSIRRNZIMVI. SKIUI'H E WMPQ VERRIG "QUNZKSMIHH," QTS NS GPIHM'S DPUW.

—ZERREZKIU

369

CBADT J FWZJD AX J SBPPACIG VAMMARNIS SPJVB, XADRB AS RWDXAXSX QPADRAQJIIG WM VBJIADT FASO ZBD.

—KWXBQO RWDPJV

367 B represents A — 368 P represents O — 369 V represents D

367

There are no innocent bystanders. What were they doing there in the first place?

—William S. Burroughs

368

I wish there was a knob on the TV to turn up the intelligence. There's a knob called "brightness," but it doesn't work.

—Gallagher

369

Being a woman is a terribly difficult trade, since it consists principally of dealing with men.

—Joseph Conrad

370

R HMB ZYRQVYJ R SMG CXHYTXZG, IYUJYWYUREQY, REH ZM ZDUE RUMDEH ZVUYY ZXNYJ SYCMUY TGXEB HMLE.

—UMSYUZ SYEQVTYG

371

AJ SKHTGDQ VFGRBVINNJ PGQBR BKIHZ F MFJ, JKI UFJ PCPDRIFNNJ QPR RK AP F AKZZ FDM SKHT RSPNCP BKIHZ F MFJ.

—HKAPHR VHKZR

372

NXC TCAETUCT RECG HEN SHRCTGNQHR NXQN JCEJMC BESMR TQNXCT PC BTEHV QHR KEUAETNQPMC NXQH TOVXN OH FQOM.

—AOHMCW JCNCT RSHHC

370

A dog teaches a boy fidelity, perseverance, and to turn around three times before lying down.

—Robert Benchley

371

By working faithfully eight hours a day, you may eventually get to be a boss and work twelve hours a day.

—Robert Frost

372

The reformer does not understand that people would rather be wrong and comfortable than right in jail.

—Finley Peter Dunne

373

LHLC ZMRXMWXH NDRX LW EZUFW FZTJW, DMX DE WJX TUXLWXFW NLGDU-FLRZMT CLYJZMXF WJX SDUNH XRXU FLS.

—BDFJ GZNNZMTF

374

YSRTR XTR CVTR CRG YSXG PVCRG AG CRGYXM SVZLAYXMZ—PSAES IWZY DVRZ YV ZSVP PSV'Z QTAFAGD PSV ETXOH.

—LRYRT FRXMR

375

CSM OMQFFR KOVDSCMZVZD CSVZD QYJNC TVBBFM QDM VG CSM EZJHFMBDM CSQC RJN'FF DOJH JNC JK VC.

—BJOVG BQR

373 R represents V

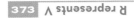

374 T represents R

375 J represents O

373

Adam invented love at first sight, one of the greatest labor-saving machines the world ever saw.

—Josh Billings

374

There are more men than women in mental hospitals—which just goes to show who's driving who crazy.

—Peter Veale

375

The really frightening thing about middle age is the knowledge that you'll grow out of it.

—Doris Day

376

QR QCUPAG WBA EVA OPDJ EVAR GVCS PD MBPGCDG WDJ CD WPBMIWDAG KALWNGA DCKCJR LWD IAWUA.

—KNBE BARDCIJG

377

JBGYBWBGULPB KY RCB CUGI XFGA EFV IF UNRBG EFV HBR RKGBI FN IFKLH RCB CUGI XFGA EFV UQGBUIE IKI.

—LBXR HKLHGKPC

378

GO GJ ECDZO OH MD Z MQHTAD. VGOP QHV DSXDLOZOGHTJ GO'J RDCU DZJU OH JWCXCGJD XDHXQD.

—XZKDQZ ZTADCJHT

376 P represents I

377 C represents H

378 X represents P

376

My movies are the kind they show in prisons and on airplanes because nobody can leave.

—Burt Reynolds

377

Perseverance is the hard work you do after you get tired of doing the hard work you already did.

—Newt Gingrich

378

It is great to be a blonde. With low expectations it's very easy to surprise people.

—Pamela Anderson

379

UW RQTRBY DG U LUW VZF ZUG LUJR UNN YZR LDGYUXRG VZDPZ PUW HR LUJR DW U ORBS WUBBFV ADRNJ.

—WDRNG HFZB

380

T DOBZ O SXU XP DXJZF, NQU T GXJ'U VOJU UX UOSB ONXQU UWOU. T VXYB MZYF WOYG OJG T'D VXYUW ZMZYF AZJU.

—JOXDT AODKNZSS

381

GM NESY HYAYI CEYR FQPXW JYI FDY. RJY KXRW WYCCR YAYIMPHY RJY'R FR PCL FR E FG. WJYH RJY CEYR FQPXW GM FDY.

—IPQYIW PIQYH

379 L represents M 380 Z represents E 381 P represents O

379

An expert is a man who has made all the mistakes which can be made in a very narrow field.

—Niels Bohr

380

I make a lot of money, but I don't want to talk about that. I work very hard and I'm worth every cent.

—Naomi Campbell

381

My wife never lies about her age. She just tells everyone she's as old as I am. Then she lies about my age.

—Robert Orben

382

EOB GBACWY YJQ CL J YDBE DG JMZJQG BJGDBI EOJW EOB LDIGE. SQ EOB GBACWY YJQ QCT'IB CLL DE.

—XJAFDB VMBJGCW

383

FK'P TFPUXNVGMFHM KX KQFHI QXE ZGHA OYXODY GVY PQXUIYT LA QXHYPKA, GHT QXE JYE LA TYUYFK.

—HXYD UXEGVT

384

BE BCDVFQ MVF IWABRI BPFCD VYI FME PFFRI YI BUTFID BI PBO BI B TFDVAQ MVF DBURI BPFCD VAQ FME JVYUOQAE.

—PAEGBTYE OYIQBAUY

382 Y represents D 383 T represents D 384 A represents E

382

The second day of a diet is always easier than the first. By the second day you're off it.

—Jackie Gleason

383

It's discouraging to think how many people are shocked by honesty, and how few by deceit.

—Noël Coward

384

An author who speaks about his own books is almost as bad as a mother who talks about her own children.

—Benjamin Disraeli

385

LA P QAQLRRX TF ENZB P ELBV VF UZV CPT FJ AFGZFBZ ENFAZ KFBHZCALVPFB SFCZA GZ, P WCZVZBT VF LUCZZ.

—LRSZCV KLGQA

386

ZXZ-SXXQH DTFZQ FD'H HFPPV DX FZAJHD DIX TXRCH' IXCQ FZ DIX KFZRDJH' JZMXVKJZD; GRD FY SXXQFZW FH JAOZJHSJZD, HX FH DTJ GOPPJD.

—MRPFO STFPL

387

FBA IAZF SANZEHA PQ N SNT'Z BPTAZFJ LZT'F BLZ LTDPSA FNM HAFEHT. LF'Z FBA YAHP NUCEZF PT BLZ INFBHPPS ZDNGA.

—NHFBEH D. DGNHXA

385 A represents S

386 Q represents K

387 L represents I

385

As I usually do when I want to get rid of someone whose conversation bores me, I pretend to agree.

—Albert Camus

386

Non-cooks think it's silly to invest two hours' work in two minutes' enjoyment; but if cooking is evanescent, so is the ballet.

—Julia Child

387

The best measure of a man's honesty isn't his income tax return. It's the zero adjust on his bathroom scale.

—Arthur C. Clarke

388

MLDR NKFNTONDHN EYI ZYJREZ XN ZEYZ OD NDRMYDS DLCLSU RLNI ZL ZEN ZENYZNT JDMNII EN LT IEN EYI CTLDHEOZOI.

—GYXNI YRYZN

389

DMYPW JNMTYKMPL YT QYHM NXPPYPW F EMUMLMNV; VAX'ZM WAL F QAL AI JMAJQM XPKMN VAX FPK PADAKV'T QYTLMPYPW.

—DYQQ EQYPLAP

390

FDBE NXE QWGV XRWLXGN JRGE XFFXTA QDBR FDBE'MB TJMRBMBV. W NKCCJNB FDXF'N QDE LE PJGVHWND QXN NJ TXGL QDBR W HGKNDBV DWL.

—QWGG PWGGBNCWB

388 M represents L

389 T represents S

390 L represents M

388

Long experience has taught me that in England nobody goes to the theater unless he or she has bronchitis.

—James Agate

389

Being president is like running a cemetery; you've got a lot of people under you and nobody's listening.

—Bill Clinton

390

They say wild animals only attack when they're cornered. I suppose that's why my goldfish was so calm when I flushed him.

—Will Gillespie

391

K AUWFGI TWJ JDGO AW NFHU DVWFJ NRAMGB KB JUMSM XMSM DTRVWIR MGAM XUWN K OTMX DA XMGG.

—UMTSR IDZKI JUWSMDF

392

AWF AWOMQ TOAW SDFAFMKOMQ XJI'DF OM Y QJJK UJJK OH AWYA HJUFAOUFH XJI RYM YRAIYNNX ADORV XJIDHFNC OMAJ CFFNOMQ EFAAFD.

—RWYDNFH KF NOMA

393

G MV QLNLHVGOLQ VZ BEGTQHLO JL JHAICEN ID GO NELGH RMNELH'F HLTGCGAO, GR NELZ BMO RGOQ AIN SEMN GN GF.

—BEMHTLF TMVJ

391 D represents A

392 K represents D

393 R represents F

391

I should not talk so much about myself if there were anybody else whom I knew as well.

—Henry David Thoreau

392

The thing with pretending you're in a good mood is that sometimes you can actually trick yourself into feeling better.

—Charles de Lint

393

I am determined my children be brought up in their father's religion, if they can find out what it is.

—Charles Lamb

394

FUNM SJ YTH CNHBYHJY YTSPC SP YTH FUNIK. JU FH JTUQIK JBEH JUWH UZ SY ZUN YUWUNNUF.

—KUP THNUIK

395

R SZH CE Z QZDL YLTLEDIU, ZEQ DBL MWU DCCA FL BCYHLGZTA YRQREM. DBZD SZH AREQ CX XWE, WEDRI SL YZE CWD CX VWZYDLYH.

—HWHRL ICWTAH

396

T OMXLPLNI TPPLPKEI JLSS RMP XMSNI TSS CMKB OBMYSIVX, YKP LP JLSS TRRMC IRMKZF OIMOSI PM VTAI LP JMBPF PFI IGGMBP.

—FIBV TSYBLZFP

394 F represents W 395 Q represents D 396 R represents N

394

Work is the greatest thing in the world. So we should save some of it for tomorrow.

—Don Herold

395

I was on a date recently, and the guy took me horseback riding. That was kind of fun, until we ran out of quarters.

—Susie Loucks

396

A positive attitude will not solve all your problems, but it will annoy enough people to make it worth the effort.

—Herm Albright

397

ZDX VTZMFHZX OJHT JL ZDX XIVQHZMJKHT GCGZXF MG ZJ GDMLZ ZJ ZDX MKIMWMIVHT ZDX NVAIXK JL UVAGVMKO DMG XIVQHZMJK.

—PJDK OHAIKXA

398

YJTA BJTE XOGG BJT SZGG LA BJT CTAOBT, BJT CTAOBZSC WZ AZB IAZY YJTBJTS BZ OACYTS "KSTCTAB" ZS "AZB VQLGBE."

—BJTZWZST SZZCTRTGB

399

FCRFRIMB INSFYNGNMB HPD GRCS: ERK SLWE SRAMX BNB XRL SPQM YPIH XMPC? SPNY NH NA.

—IHPAHRA BMYPFYPAM

397 I represents D 398 O represents A 399 F represents P

397

The ultimate goal of the educational system is to shift to the individual the burden of pursuing his education.

—John Gardner

398

When they call the roll in the Senate, the Senators do not know whether to answer "Present" or "Not Guilty."

—Theodore Roosevelt

399

Proposed simplified tax form: How much money did you make last year? Mail it in.

—Stanton Delaplane

400

M'X HCC MT DHBJQ JD WRRNMTL YHTLRQJEV ARHNJTV JEK JD KZR ZHTYV JD DJJCV. CRK'V VKHQK AMKZ KPNRAQMKRQV.

—VJCJXJT VZJQK

401

E SKEQLSA OEQK ERVQL HUMK TUDGVOKG KETS AKEM UDK EDR E SEQY LZOKG SZG UXD XKZFSL ZD ULSKM NKUNQK'G NELZKDTK.

—PUSD VNRZCK

402

VSVZF IWB PWK W ZOTPQ QA DQQVZ XPWQ PV QPOBJK QZDQP, WBR VSVZF AQPVZ IWB PWK W ZOTPQ QA JBAEJ POI RAXB GAZ OQ.

—KWIDVY MAPBKAB

400 K represents T — 401 Q represents L — 402 A represents O

400

I'm all in favor of keeping dangerous weapons out of the hands of fools. Let's start with typewriters.

—Solomon Short

401

A healthy male adult bore consumes each year one and a half times his own weight in other people's patience.

—John Updike

402

Every man has a right to utter what he thinks truth, and every other man has a right to knock him down for it.

—Samuel Johnson

403

EGN TYEYON, RPPFOUSHQ EF VFZN VPSNHESVEV, LSAA IN NDRPEAX ASBN EGN JRVE, FHAX TRO ZFON NDJNHVSMN.

—KFGH EGFZRV VARUNB

404

MRX NXOLVS IRK LV JXI WVVA PVVFL ONX INHMMXS HL MROM LV JXI CXVCYX IRV EOS INHMX FSVI OSKMRHSW.

—IOYMXN POWXRVM

405

WL AHI PQFX AHIY BJWGSYKF XH WRMYHEK, GKX XJKR HEKYJKQY XJK FWBK XJWFDU AHI UQA QTHIX XJKR XH HXJKYU.

—JQWR DWFHXX

403 P represents C 404 N represents R 405 H represents O

403

The future, according to some scientists, will be exactly like the past, only far more expensive.

—John Thomas Sladek

404

The reason why so few good books are written is that so few people who can write know anything.

—Walter Bagehot

405

If you want your children to improve, let them overhear the nice things you say about them to others.

—Haim Ginott

406

EOWOA KFAAT SZFJQ QPO HXNO FL TFJA VPAXHQCSH QAOO. XE QPO OTOH FL VPXIBAOE, QPOT SAO SII QPXAQT LOOQ QSII.

—ISAAT KXIBO

407

DJIGZ UZC LURF DNHH CJ UF RMGB OHGUFG, UZC IGZ UZC CJAF FMJQHC VGHUY UZC AGR QFGC RJ RMG NCGU.

—VJKGVR U. MGNZHGNZ

408

WZU VMH OK ZOGH V CZVBH TZFOBM LQDWAMQ V KLWDI. WBXH FWA'DH VEWVDU, LQHDH'K BWLQOBM FWA XVB UW VEWAL OL.

—MWZUV IHOD

406 S represents A **407** C represents D **408** H represents E

406

Never worry about the size of your Christmas tree. In the eyes of children, they are all thirty feet tall.

—Larry Wilde

407

Women and cats will do as they please, and men and dogs should relax and get used to the idea.

—Robert A. Heinlein

408

Old age is like a plane flying through a storm. Once you're aboard, there's nothing you can do about it.

—Golda Meir

409

NJDCDNDPB, YDSR JUDL, PQXKYO HR TRLCYR RLXKTQ CX LXKJDPQ U BUL'P TJXECQ EDCQXKC ORPCJXADLT QDP JXXCP.

—WJULS U. NYUJS

410

HCREXVZVPA FK I YIA VG VMPIXFUFXP HEC BXFJCMKC KV HEIH NIX LVCKX'H EIJC HV CODCMFCXRC FH.

—NIO GMFKRE

411

OKMMVXF DVUX WXKELXJ SBX VBPKDZKCDX DXJJSB: WS WLVBH SU WLVBAJ UKM XBSZAL KLXKF BSW WS JKR WLXO.

—IXUUXMJSB OKELKOXM

409 T represents G

410 I represents A

411 L represents H

409

Criticism, like rain, should be gentle enough to nourish a man's growth without destroying his roots.

—Frank A. Clark

410

Technology is a way of organizing the universe so that man doesn't have to experience it.

—Max Frisch

411

Married life teaches one invaluable lesson: to think of things far enough ahead not to say them.

—Jefferson Machamer

412

EH TDMW TDQ BTXMS RQMM RNXQ MTLQ HNTP HFMCQ MTLQ FC TDQ BFD RQMM PXCVNTTPC HNTP RTFSCRTTMC.

—GFRVFNEDQ PFDCHEQMS

413

NIRMQTWTFUREW HOTFOICC MEC SIOIWZ HOTPUVIV JC DUNM STOI IBBURUIQN SIEQC BTO FTUQF LERYDEOVC.

—EWVTJC MJKWIZ

414

MPJAVYM JXF VW XVNB ZBVYM VYSPBOWVYMXC KBYOXVDBF LJP O SPVUB CJE GOQBY'I SJUUVIIBF.

—OYIGJYC KJABXX

412 R represents T 413 R represents C 414 J represents O

412

If only one could tell true love from false love as one can tell mushrooms from toadstools.

—Katharine Mansfield

413

Technological progress has merely provided us with more efficient means for going backwards.

—Aldous Huxley

414

Growing old is like being increasingly penalized for a crime you haven't committed.

—Anthony Powell

415

WP GWPU LUEU AMJB, LU LVMGZ CU CVEF VGZ XFZ XRYWUSU KVMBY XCVMB BYU BWIU LU'Z JXSUZ UFVMOY BV UFAVK WB.

—AWI PWUCWO

416

USIVKSV KWKUXKCUXUVE OUVZLGV HLSIVKSV QJAIASHA UI QJLCKCXE VZA CAIV JLXA K FLVZAJ HKS QXKE.

—XLVVA CKUXES

417

SOPXZM EPO ECJEZO: PO XIZV FRAOY YCGGOYY DPOI PO YEWGAY PWY IOGA XCE.

—HRFOY SJVRIE GXIRIE

415 Y represents H

416 Q represents P

417 C represents U

415

If life were just, we would be born old and achieve youth about the time we'd saved enough to enjoy it.

—Jim Fiebig

416

Instant availability without constant presence is probably the best role a mother can play.

—Lotte Bailyn

417

Behold the turtle: he only makes success when he sticks his neck out.

—James Bryant Conant

418

BFT PZQI TZL VRWQ OD KZJPI FVZTQ, PQIXRLQ LGQ EFML LGFL IZBQLRBQI GQ GFI LZ QFL LGQB.

—FPVFR ILQWQTIZT

419

ZCVGDGFGLJM BEC FCRZVLGJ LOCKD DEI RIPGL LHI VGSI MLGVCHM BEC FCRZVLGJ LOCKD DEI MIL.

—IJCFE ZCBIVV

420

D VX YLP V SBRBPVNDVY FBEVWOB D QLSB VVYDXVQO; D VX V SBRBPVNDVY FBEVWOB D GVPB UQVYPO.

—V. AGDPYBC FNLAY

418 B represents M

419 I represents E

420 B represents E

418

Man does not live by words alone, despite the fact that sometimes he has to eat them.

—Adlai Stevenson

419

Politicians who complain about the media are like sailors who complain about the sea.

—Enoch Powell

420

I am not a vegetarian because I love animals; I am a vegetarian because I hate plants.

—A. Whitney Brown

421

LKIGB SHI'Z PFB BKF UHTTYIGEE, PFZ YZ SHI PFB BKF H BHSUZ PYW GIKFWU ZK TFXX FT DYWUZ HXKIWEYJG YZ.

—JHRYJ XGG DKZU

422

ICC VIKKXIZWE IKW LIFFS. XN'E NKSXBZ NQ CXDW NQZWNLWK IJNWKAIKGE NLIN MITEWE ICC NLW FKQOCWVE.

—ELWCCWS AXBNWKE

423

BR CBUC BUG KA LAAIG, WKUXRG KAT ZRQQUTG SK BSG LUESIJ OUG ZRQAC ZJ U LIUGB AL ISQBCKSKQ.

—CBAEUG LMIIRT

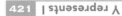

421 Y represents I 422 C represents L 423 L represents F

421

Money can't buy you happiness, but it can buy you a yacht big enough to pull up right alongside it.

—David Lee Roth

422

All marriages are happy. It's trying to live together afterwards that causes all the problems.

—Shelley Winters

423

He that has no fools, knaves nor beggars in his family was begot by a flash of lightning.

—Thomas Fuller

424

PZAAXFZZU CK V GAVTS FPSIS EPSX GAVTS XZJ JDUSI TZDEIVTE CDKESVU ZN JDUSI ZYKSIHVECZD.

—FVAESI FCDTPSAA

425

O QUFL IOXMBFLKLI WQUW UHH QSRUP LFOH MBRLX AKBR WQOX: RUP'X NLOPY SPUNHL WB XOW XWOHH OP U KBBR.

—NHUOXL ZUXMUH

426

DXTTGDP RG NB N'R KTXLA, HOP UZVL'P PUG BNLG YNLG HGPKGGL VZLNPE ZLS RZSLGVV AXPPGL BNLGT?

—AGXTAG WTNDG

424 X represents Y

425 L represents E

426 R represents M

424

Hollywood is a place where they place you under contract instead of under observation.

—Walter Winchell

425

I have discovered that all human evil comes from this: man's being unable to sit still in a room.

—Blaise Pascal

426

Correct me if I'm wrong, but hasn't the fine line between sanity and madness gotten finer?

—George Price

427

YB QBI VBQYTEQ ILT ASYJETQI BU NQBILTD CTVNSRT GI YGUUTDR UDBE HBSD BKQ. HBS ENH CBIL CT KDBQJ.

—YNQYTEGR

428

CYGC ZK CXH YTC RW OYDZJS SAHKCK WHHEYC XROH PXHJ CXYC'K THYEEV PXHTH VRA PZKX CXHV PHTH.

—SHRTSH H. IHTSOYJ

429

ON XSAQA'M BTFVTA GOMXATOTD XV LSVY O VLA YVTAF, O'Y CQACBQAZ XV NVQDAX OX ON FVK BQA.

—AQQVG NGFTT

427 N represents A | 428 P represents W | 429 Y represents M

427

Do not condemn the judgment of another because it differs from your own. You may both be wrong.

—Dandemis

428

Tact is the art of making guests feel at home when that's really where you wish they were.

—George E. Bergman

429

If there's anyone listening to whom I owe money, I'm prepared to forget it if you are.

—Errol Flynn

430

MYV DVMMVS XV KVVF WDRBM RBSTVFQVT, MYV KVXVS MUEVT XV YWQV MR PHRZP TREVDRJL VFTV JRXH MR KVVF MWFF.

—RJVMMW

431

CY AUP XZWRX WKWZA TCXPRXCUG RT R SCYW-RGB-BWRXD ORXXWZ, AUP'SS BCW R SUX UY XCOWT.

—BWRG TOCXD

432

WM DUOBP JRKBCWUO YROR GWDAPQ MUPPUYWXN OSPRG, YR TUSPI AOUNOBD B TUDASFRO FU JR DUOBP.

—GBDSRP A. NWXIRO

430 R represents O

431 X represents T

432 A represents P

430

The better we feel about ourselves, the fewer times we have to knock somebody else down to feel tall.

—Odetta

431

If you treat every situation as a life-and-death matter, you'll die a lot of times.

—Dean Smith

432

If moral behavior were simply following rules, we could program a computer to be moral.

—Samuel P. Ginder

433

SXNWN ICGS ON GUINSXJAQ SU ZHCVCAHSCWN–ZDSNW ZRR, EUC ANLNW GNN ZAE GJHT VUWHCVJANG.

—OUO QUMMZWM

434

NABHGA PHCY JAHJEA CYUGY NHUCYXID UNHRY YWAXG BUPXEZ YGAA, YWAZ RCRUEEZ MH U DHHM JGRIXID VHN.

—H.U. NUYYXCYU

435

BZPZOW DYXX LHLT DYB SNL PUSSXL ZM SNL ELVLE. SNLTL'E SZZ AIQN MTUSLTBYRYBJ DYSN SNL LBLAW.

—NLBTW FYEEYBJLT

433 C represents U

434 J represents P

435 Z represents O

433

There must be something to acupuncture—after all, you never see any sick porcupines.

—Bob Goddard

434

Before most people start boasting about their family tree, they usually do a good pruning job.

—O.A. Battista

435

Nobody will ever win the battle of the sexes. There's too much fraternizing with the enemy.

—Henry Kissinger

436

WJBC KENT IQJ CERTD IQJ'ON VSYFJYCNF GSQH CEN BZEQQM QG NAUNSRNTZN, BQHNQTN CERTDB JU Y TNK ZQJSBN.

—HYSI E. KYMFSRU

437

N XOSL JNGECSLYLJ ZXL OYZ CU JLELNSNBI JNMHCVOZG. N ZLHH ZXLV ZXL ZYWZX OBJ ZXLF BLSLY TLHNLSL VL.

—EOVNHHC JN EOSCWY

438

GLV SKG QFDOE DQ'P K YLOU HKG JLHO QFX TLKJ QL QFX JTVU PQLTX, MVQ QFKQ'P WVPQ ZXKOVQP QL PZKRX.

—JLVUYKP KJKSP

436 Z represents C

437 S represents V

438 J represents D

436

Just when you think you've graduated from the school of experience, someone thinks up a new course.

—Mary H. Waldrip

437

I have discovered the art of deceiving diplomats. I tell them the truth and they never believe me.

—Camillo di Cavour

438

You may think it's a long way down the road to the drug store, but that's just peanuts to space.

—Douglas Adams

439

ZCDZOC XBD TVFC BKRPDQL FIDX IDPBKIU VMDNP BKRPDQL. LDN WVI RCC PBVP KI PBC RDQP DS BKRPDQL PBCL TVFC.

—U.F. WBCRPCQPDI

440

KJUNIJ O ENS AGIIOJR, O CGR MOD SCJNIOJM GKNWS KIOVEOVE WH FCOPRIJV; VNQ O CGBJ MOD FCOPRIJV GVR VN SCJNIOJM.

—ZNCV QOPANS

441

M OML IUT SNQIW CUQ ITEPJ CUQ WMOQ MC YNYCX MW UQ JNJ MC CIQLCX UMW IMWCQJ CUNECX XQMEW TY UNW PNYQ.

—OFUMOOMJ MPN

439 L represents Y

440 G represents A

441 I represents W

439

People who make history know nothing about history. You can see that in the sort of history they make.

—G.K. Chesterton

440

Before I got married, I had six theories about bringing up children; now I have six children and no theories.

—John Wilmot

441

A man who views the world the same at fifty as he did at twenty has wasted thirty years of his life.

—Muhammad Ali

442

SV Y PORROJ-XJAOJOA UXJQA, RMO LZEGZ TXRM UXFQA GMXU FE SV XIRXPOJ YVA OYR RMO QOYKOG YNROJ RMOZ'KO NYQQOV.

—OAUYJA GROKOVGXV

443

GNS ZAAKDWZSKQQU DBVGRQN ZS BCN BPVBC, RVB GZDB ZL BCNG EWAI BCNGDNQMND VE KSX CVPPU ZLL KD WL SZBCWSJ CKX CKEENSNX.

—FWSDBZS ACVPACWQQ

444

DGXAWIHRMJGX, ONJDN JH HQBBGHWK MG SW R MOG-ORT HMIWWM, JH MIWRMWK ST URXT RH JY JM OWIW R KJAJKWK NJVNORT.

—UJHH URXXWIH

442 Q represents L

443 G represents M

444 I represents R

442

In a better-ordered world, the gypsy moth would show up in October and eat the leaves after they've fallen.

—Edward Stevenson

443

Men occasionally stumble on the truth, but most of them pick themselves up and hurry off as if nothing had happened.

—Winston Churchill

444

Conversation, which is supposed to be a two-way street, is treated by many as if it were a divided highway.

—Miss Manners

445

XRFVYKJL RZPJ LJPJK SJJL PJKW NMMY ZB VFABJLFLN BM BRJFK JVYJKA, SQB BRJW RZPJ LJPJK DZFVJY BM FUFBZBJ BRJU.

—CZUJA SZVYEFL

446

NJHEQ DK H ZJWB NSTT, NWJHWB HIIHDW, HGN RB HNZDLJ EU BUS DK EU QHZJ GUEQDGY PQHEJZJW EU NU PDEQ DE.

—P. KURJWKJE RHSYQHR

447

AC GXNJC IEXYCWQCY IL IEX USNWNRT RI VCR U GNFFU RI IEX JIIX OUYRCX RKUL UL UDSEWULHC.

—ANWW JEXYR

445 P represents V | 446 U represents O | 447 R represents T

445

Children have never been very good at listening to their elders, but they have never failed to imitate them.

—James Baldwin

446

Death is a very dull, dreary affair, and my advice to you is to have nothing whatever to do with it.

—W. Somerset Maugham

447

We pride ourselves on our ability to get a pizza to our door faster than an ambulance.

—Will Durst

448

E GYRHZERHG VYPJHO ES ZNH RQPBSQIZBOHOG YS SYYAWOYYS EZHRG THHW Q SYYA YO ZVY YP ZNHEO WQFOYAA ZY ZHGZ ZNEPCG.

—QAQP IYOHP

449

AR UYGEFP QD RDI EL TPQ AUXXEPY: EM RDI MEHY U TDDY SEMP RDI'OO CP JUWWR; EM HDQ, RDI SEOO CPFDAP U WJEODLDWJPX.

—LDFXUQPL

450

KR UWFH JLHZV NZVZUVLWISH KU QWV ZQQWGQNHX HPHLM FWLQKQJ, YH RHHT Z NHLVZKQ PWKX. QWVSKQJ KQ VSH IZIHL VWXZM, YH UKJS.

—TWLX ZNVWQ

448 R represents M

449 M represents F

450 N represents C

448

I sometimes wonder if the manufacturers of foolproof items keep a fool or two on their payroll to test things.

—Alan Coren

449

My advice to you is get married: if you find a good wife you'll be happy; if not, you will become a philosopher.

—Socrates

450

If some great catastrophe is not announced every morning, we feel a certain void. Nothing in the paper today, we sigh.

—Lord Acton

451

QVZ FZIP TYP RDCVWCYO PV ALCY LD RFKLJP. DV VDY RI RFKMYIIYO GRPA PAY GVD-WVIP MYJVMO VU PAY MYUYMYY.

—XVAD A. AVWJVFH

452

QE QL G HOZGE SZTX YDO G AGW ED CZ QW TDNZ MQES SQALZTY. YDO GW GREDO, SDMZNZO, QE QL GCLDTJEZTI ZLLZWEQGT.

—ODCZOE ADOTZI

453

UOXZX JZX UOZXX EUJPXE CS KJW: OX HXRTXAXE TW EJWUJ NRJME, OX QCXE WCU HXRTXAX TW EJWUJ NRJME, OX TE EJWUJ NRJME.

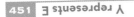

—HCH DOTRRTDE

451 Y represents E

452 S represents H

453 U represents T

451

You must get involved to have an impact. No one is impressed with the won-lost record of the referee.

—John H. Holcomb

452

It is a great help for a man to be in love with himself. For an actor, however, it is absolutely essential.

—Robert Morley

453

There are three stages of man: he believes in Santa Claus, he does not believe in Santa Claus, he is Santa Claus.

—Bob Phillips

454

IUH IARGYDH PFIU IHDDFWK Q KRRN JIRAV FJ IUQI FI FWMQAFQYDV AHXFWNJ IUH RIUHA EHDDRP RE Q NGDD RWH.

—JFN SQHJQA

455

BRAAVJB KJ VERK HQZTIE LR IVOR HVAAVJB ZJ K MVJ. VA HQZTIE CKOR PZT WTCM TM KJE EZ HZCRAQVJB.

—R.I. HVCMHZJ

456

JM GME DMVVU TOMRE UMRV WVMONPIC DZEA ITEAPITEZKC; Z TCCRVP UMR IZGP TVP BTV SVPTEPV.

—TNOPVE PZGCEPZG

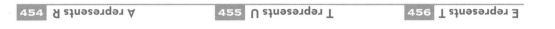

454 A represents R

455 T represents U

456 E represents T

454

The trouble with telling a good story is that it invariably reminds the other fellow of a dull one.

—Sid Caesar

455

Getting an idea should be like sitting on a pin. It should make you jump up and do something.

—E.L. Simpson

456

Do not worry about your problems with mathematics; I assure you mine are far greater.

—Albert Einstein

457

WA WF HOART YIGC AH CWFAWTXZWFY VRALRRT AYR BTHMBF HO EWOR ITC AYHFR HO HNNHGAZTWAQ.

—OGRCRGWMB NYWEEWNF

458

CGGCFVQWZVO ZI EZIINX HO ECIV GNCGUN HNBDQIN ZV ZI XFNIINX ZW CYNFDUUI DWX UCCRI UZRN LCFR.

—VMCEDI NXZICW

459

ZWM YGXI ZWNGS ZWLZ VYGZNGKMA ZY SNTM KA UYJM CYJ YKJ UYGMI NA ZWM DMNSWNGS ULVWNGM.

—SMYJSM VXLJO

457 R represents E

458 C represents O

459 G represents N

457

It is often hard to distinguish between the knocks of life and those of opportunity.

—Frederick Phillips

458

Opportunity is missed by most people because it is dressed in overalls and looks like work.

—Thomas Edison

459

The only thing that continues to give us more for our money is the weighing machine.

—George Clark

460

OEIJ, WLDJRSZGDH, LJZHJTV SE REV PRDVJ HJEHOJ NZ KPTG NZ N TEKKER GNVLJS WEL ZEKJVGDRY.

—NRVER TGJQGEI

461

KJW SEQRK XEXWVK HEQ CV CKJWMRK MR SJWV JW HWWNR LQCKWHDN CVO JCR VE EVW KE KJCVF.

—SWVOG SCQO

462

LG SWMLOLZQ, LC EWH IDGO DGEONLGX QDLF, DQV D KDG; LC EWH IDGO DGEONLGX FWGJ, DQV D IWKDG.

—KDPXDPJO ONDOZNJP

460 G represents H 461 H represents F 462 I represents W

460

Love, friendship, respect do not unite people as much as a common hatred for something.

—Anton Chekhov

461

The worst moment for an atheist is when he feels grateful and has no one to thank.

—Wendy Ward

462

In politics, if you want anything said, ask a man; if you want anything done, ask a woman.

—Margaret Thatcher

463

APM LBFEMEA AF QMGTMLAVFR I QMGEFR MXMG LFHME VE NPMR PM TVBBE FZA I KFO IQQBVLIAVFR TFGH.

—EAIRBMC K. GIRSIBB

464

JD RIFVIE VIYR JO VI HVIC QMUAZN AZVAJMVO RAZZOEH SIE SIWE. WZYOHH VQOEO MEO VQEOO IVQOE COICYO.

—IEHIZ LOYYOH

465

GH'T B ZSMSTTGPW ALSW IPCZ WSGDLEPZ UPTST LGT KPE; GH'T B RSXZSTTGPW ALSW IPC UPTS IPCZ PAW.

—LBZZI T. HZCFBW

463 T represents F 464 Z represents N 465 L represents H

463

The closest to perfection a person ever comes is when he fills out a job application form.

—Stanley J. Randall

464

My doctor told me to stop having intimate dinners for four. Unless there are three other people.

—Orson Welles

465

It's a recession when your neighbor loses his job; it's a depression when you lose your own.

—Harry S. Truman

466

R NWJRS XRYK TJHTBJ SCZYD SCJK RWJ SCZYDZYN QCJY SCJK RWJ XJWJBK WJRWWRYNZYN SCJZW TWJAMOZPJL.

—QZBBZRX ARXJL

467

B XALBE RV UROK B HKB SBM—JAF WBE'H HKUU PAX VHQAEM VPK RV FEHRU JAF IFH PKQ RE PAH XBHKQ.

—EBEWJ QKBMBE

468

VUPQBTCZJN XZUBRI SR KP ZER HUJR, VTZ GPR ZEGTYEZ QRCZ SR JUOS; XGGP K'I VR ZGG CGGB ZG PRRI UP UPZK-ZERHZ UOUBS.

—YKPU BGZEHROX

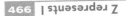

466 Z represents I | 467 U represents L | 468 J represents C

466

A great many people think they are thinking when they are merely rearranging their prejudices.

—William James

467

A woman is like a tea bag—you can't tell how strong she is until you put her in hot water.

—Nancy Reagan

468

Bankruptcy stared me in the face, but one thought kept me calm; soon I'd be too poor to need an anti-theft alarm.

—Gina Rothfels

469

G YQUVRO AOQAYO XRQ HOOA TQDC. VROI ULO EQXULTC XRQ RUWOK'V DQV VRO DFVC VQ PGVO AOQAYO VROJCOYWOC.

—UFDFCV CVLGKTPOLD

470

P MPYF RJIJWPZPBY WJDK JFHXGRPYU. JWJDK RPNJ ZBNJEBFK RHDYZ BY RSJ ZJR, P UB PYRB RSJ BRSJD DBBN GYF DJGF G EBBV.

—UDBHXSB NGDO

471

UQHM KQAROMU ZCNQDKM SMKPAUM QG P HCUALZMDUVPLZCLT; QVIMDU, SMKPAUM VIMB ALZMDUVPLZ MPKI QVIMD VQQ JMOO.

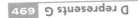

—MNPL MUPD

469 D represents G 470 N represents M 471 K represents C

469

I loathe people who keep dogs. They are cowards who haven't got the guts to bite people themselves.

—August Strindberg

470

I find television very educating. Every time somebody turns on the set, I go into the other room and read a book.

—Groucho Marx

471

Some couples divorce because of a misunderstanding; others, because they understand each other too well.

—Evan Esar

472

HPGBG VN WRAO WRG EVYYGBGRXG KGHJGGR Z QZEQZR ZRE QG. HPG QZEQZR HPVRCN PG VN NZRG. V CRWJ V ZQ QZE.

—NZASZEWB EZAV

473

SPUHXLMM OM SPUWOUKBDDN BQQPOUWOUH GBSW-GOUZOUH SPVVOWWLLM, CRLU CRBW CL XLBDDN ULLZ BXL MPVL GBSW-GBSOUH SPVVOWWLLM.

—XPHLX BDDLU

474

JQWAWPY WD AOU VPST RQVIUDDWVP JOUQU PV VPU HVPDWNUQD TVB QWNWHBSVBD WI TVB UEQP PV KVPUT.

—MBSUD QUPEQN

472 R represents N   473 B represents A   474 T represents Y

472

There is only one difference between a madman and me. The madman thinks he is sane. I know I am mad.

—Salvador Dali

473

Congress is continually appointing fact-finding committees, when what we really need are some fact-facing committees.

—Roger Allen

474

Writing is the only profession where no one considers you ridiculous if you earn no money.

—Jules Renard